ON THE WAY TO EMMAUS

Five Major Messianic Prophecies Explained

ENDORSEMENTS

The book of Professor Jacques Doukhan covers a large field of biblical texts, from the first chapters of Genesis onward to a good dozen of texts and, from there, to the Septuagint, the Targums, the Dead Sea Scrolls, the Jewish traditional sources such as Midrashic and Talmudic, and the New Testament! The scope is thus all-embracing, and it is with an assured mastery that the author takes his readers through the maze of traditions rich in insights but also in potentially inner contradictions.

Another noteworthy part of the book is an insightful exposition of the hotly debated Isaiah 52–53 passage on the "Servant of the Lord." The author's mastership is here again evident and his familiarity with the Rabbinic literature proves helpful. . . . The author's exposition is consistently challenging and thought provoking. He is particularly adept in discerning the literary structure of texts and thus in highlighting their intended cores.

Professor Jacques Doukhan's book will undoubtedly address a conservative readership (that is, the major trend in modern Christianity). To more "liberal" people, like me, the challenge to their hermeneutics is welcome and of great reward. I strongly recommend the publication of Jacques Doukhan's present work.

André LaCocque
Professor Emeritus of Hebrew Bible
Chicago Theological Seminary

I have read *On the Way to Emmaus*, and I highly recommend it. The book provides a careful reading of the most important messianic prophecies in the Bible, one that will be appreciated by most Messianic Jews and sympathetic evangelical Christians. It displays solid conservative scholarship, as we would expect from a respected veteran such as Doukhan. But it also builds upon current methodologies, such as inner-biblical exegesis, to open new avenues of interpretation.

While other interpretations of these prophetic texts are possible, Doukhan offers many exegetical insights that will be of value even to those scholars who are not persuaded by his overall argument.

Rabbi Mark S. Kinzer, Ph.D.
Senior Scholar
Messianic Jewish Theological Institute

ON THE WAY TO EMMAUS

Five Major Messianic Prophecies Explained

Jacques B. Doukhan, D.Heb.Lett., Th.D.

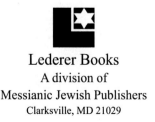

Lederer Books
A division of
Messianic Jewish Publishers
Clarksville, MD 21029

2015   2

Library of Congress Control Number: 2012939768

ISBN 978-1-936716-43-2

Printed in the United States of America

Copyright © 2012 by Jacques B. Doukhan, D.Heb.Lett., Th.D.

Published by

Lederer Books

A division of

Messianic Jewish Publishers

6120 Day Long Lane

Clarksville, Maryland 21029

Distributed by

Messianic Jewish Resources Int'l.

www.messianicjewish.net

Individual and Trade Order line: 800-410-7367

Email: lederer@messianicjewish.net

CONTENTS

FOREWORD

I initially encountered the work of Jacques Doukhan almost ten years ago, when his fine volume, *Israel and the Church*, was first published. I was impressed by his capable scholarship and his irenic tone, but also by his clearly-defined sense of Jewish identity. Before this, I had not realized that kindred spirits to my own could be found in the Seventh-day Adventist world. Reading *Israel and the Church* opened my eyes, and my mind.

I came to know Jacques personally in the fall of 2010, and was even more impressed by the man I encountered than by the work he had produced. I found him charming, witty, erudite, and gracious. But I also found a strong-minded and passionate Jew, who loved the tradition of his people, even as he loved the Messiah whom God had sent to redeem them.

Jacques Doukham has much to offer the Messianic Jewish world, and those Christian friends who support it. What he has to offer is well-displayed in this current volume. *On the Way to Emmaus* provides a careful and insightful reading of the most important messianic prophecies in the bible, one that will be appreciated by most Messianic Jews and sympathetic evangelical Christians. It displays solid conservative scholarship, as we would expect from a respected veteran such as Doukhan. But it also builds upon current methodologies, such as inner-biblical exegesis, to open new avenues of interpretation.

I am honored to introduce Jacques to the Messianic Jewish world, and am confident that those who come to know him and his work will be as grateful for the discovery as I have been.

Rabbi Mark S. Kinzer, Ph.D.
Senior Scholar
Messianic Jewish Theological Institute

INTRODUCTION

O n the way to Emmaus, just a few miles from Jerusalem, two friends are surprised by a stranger. He does not seem to know what has just happened and no one knows where he comes from! "Are you the only stranger in Jerusalem, and have you not known the things which happened there in these days?" they ask. To which he answers: "What things?" (Luke 24:18).

The two friends do not know the meaning of these events, nor do they know who the stranger is. They think they know, but they do not know. While the stranger, who they think does not know, knows. The story tells us that beginning with Moses and all the Prophets, he explained to them what was said in all the Scriptures concerning himself (Luke 24:27, NIV). Yet, according to the story the two friends still do not understand. In spite of this study, the first systematic lesson on what will be called the "messianic prophecies," they are still unable to know Him and get His point. The messianic prophecies, even explained by Him, are not enough to convince them.

We may then wonder whether we are not all of us, Christians and Jews, and all the others carrying the same question suspended in the void, unable to know Him. Whether we are not all, like these two friends who were disputing on

1

the way to Emmaus, disturbed by our unanswered question and troubled by our doubts (Luke 24:38). For as long as the Messiah is not here to answer Himself, we are like them. We do not know. A story is told about Martin Buber[1] addressing a group of Catholic priests. He asked them the question: "What is the difference between Jews and Christians? We all await the Messiah. You believe He has already come and gone, while we do not. I therefore propose that we await Him together. And when He appears, we can ask Him: 'Were you here before?'" Then he paused and added, "and I hope that at that moment I will be close enough to whisper in his ear, 'For the love of heaven, don't answer!'"

And it is as if the Messiah has heard Martin Buber's request: so far the Messiah has not come to answer and the question remains unanswered.

We are not sure who is right, the Christians who affirm that the Messiah has already come, or the Jews who are still waiting for Him.

For many Christians, "messianic prophecies" suggest the ultimate argument against the Jews. These biblical texts are brandished as evidence to show that Jesus of Nazareth was indeed the Messiah announced by the Hebrew Scriptures; they are the proof that He was here before. "Messianic prophecies" have then been used as a fast-food apologetic and the reason for diligently accusing the Jews of stubborn incredulity because they do not want to believe in spite of all these clear proofs.

For many Jews, the reference to "messianic prophecies" is associated with the Christians' attempt to convert them and is therefore suspect. Against the traditional Christian

---

1. Elie Wiesel, *All Rivers Run to the Sea* (New York: Knopf, 1996), 354–533.

interpretation, Jews erect then an opposing Jewish interpretation of these texts,[2] either pointing them to a past event in biblical times[3] or more generally applying to the eschatological event concluding human history. The Jews still wait for the Messiah to come to bring redemption to the world.

Messianic prophecies even bring some embarrassment to many others who are disturbed with what they consider the "naive" idea that religious truth could be established on the supernatural ground of prediction. In these times of biblical criticism and existential categories of thinking, this way of reasoning is not very popular; so for many Jews, and even Christians, the call for "messianic prophecies" is meaningless and irrelevant. Indeed, neither Jews nor Christians need the reference to these texts to ensure their respective faiths and religious identity.

Now, whether these texts raise suspicion, skepticism, or even indifference should not keep us from recognizing at least one historical fact: it is on the basis of these texts from the Torah and the prophets that many Jews were convinced by other Jews that Jesus of Nazareth was indeed the Messiah:

> Paul called the leaders of the Jews together . . . many came to him at his lodging, to whom he explained and solemnly testified of the kingdom of God, persuading them concerning Jesus from the Law of Moses and the prophets, from morning till evening.

---

2. For the Jewish interpretation of the messianic texts, see Raphael Patai's anthology of *The Messiah Texts* (Detroit, MI: Wayne State University Press, 1988).

3. One characteristic case of this trend is the Talmudic statement that "Israel has no Messiah because he was already consumed in the days of Hezekiah" (*b. Sanhedrin* 98b, 99a).

And some were persuaded by the things which were spoken, and some disbelieved." (Acts 28:17, 23–24, cf. Luke 24: 27, 44; Acts 8:35)

It is still on the basis of the interpretation of these texts that Jews and Christians depart theologically from each other.

The discussion about messianic prophecies is, therefore, an important one. It hits at the very origins of Christianity and takes us to the very heart of the early Jewish-Christian controversy. In essence, this discussion confronts us still today, Jews and Christians as well, with a hermeneutic problem: Did these texts indeed intend to point to the Messiah and more specifically to Jesus? Were the early Christians and the New Testament people "exegetically" correct in their messianic interpretation of the Old Testament texts? Unfortunately, the New Testament accounts limit themselves to referring, or only alluding to, the messianic prophecies without indicating their exegetical method. This loose exegetical methodology has exposed the New Testament authors to serious criticism. They have, then, been accused of twisting the Hebrew Scriptures.[4]

Christian interpreters are divided on that issue.[5] For most conservative Christians, the proof of messianic prophecies is established on the very fact that this is the interpretation provided by the authors of the New Testament and Jesus himself. Other Christians, however, take a more critical view on that matter and recognize the difficulty of the New

---

4. See, for instance, S. Vernon McCasland, "Matthew Twists the Scriptures," *Journal of Biblical Literature* 80 (1961): 143–148.

5. For a general outline of these positions, see Walter C. Kaiser, Jr., *The Messiah in the Old Testament* (Grand Rapids, MI: Zondervan, 1995), 18–28; cf. John H. Sailhamer, "The Messiah and the Hebrew Bible," *Journal of the Evangelical Theological Society* 44, no. 1 (March 2001): 5–23.

Testament interpretation of messianic prophecies. They then offer a variety of hypotheses. Some argue that these texts are not actual predictions, but concern instead a situation that is only contemporary (*single meaning*). According to this view, the authors of the so-called messianic prophecies did not predict about the future coming of Jesus of Nazareth but had only in mind a contemporary figure, a prophet (e.g., Isaiah), or a king (e.g., David, Hezekiah). Thus it is suggested that these texts have been given by the New Testament a new meaning altogether different from the original one (*relecture*). Others assume that these texts carry, in fact, a double meaning (*dual meaning*); namely, the historical, original meaning, referring to a contemporary figure and the prophetic, more developed, fuller meaning (*sensus plenior*), referring to the future Messiah.

The crucial problem of messianic prophecies is then essentially a hermeneutic problem, since it concerns the "exegetical" validity of the messianic interpretation of the biblical texts and comes down to that question: Did the early Christians have good exegetical reasons to apply these Old Testament texts to Jesus and then to recognize him as the Messiah predicted in the Hebrew Scriptures?

Definitions and Methods

Now, the very word "messiah," and for that matter the concept of "messianic prophecies" around which all our discussion revolves, are quite elusive and difficult to define. Before we engage in the exegetical enterprise and try to answer the above question, it is therefore important to clarify the meaning of these terms.

The word "messiah" comes from the Hebrew *mashiah*, the passive form of the Hebrew verb *mashah* meaning "to anoint." The "messiah" was the "anointed one," that is the one who was anointed with the sacred oil, a practice, which was used in ancient Israel to set apart a certain individual for the exclusive purpose of God's service or for a special mission. The term "messiah" was thus "applied predominantly to a king, but also to a priest, and occasionally to a prophet."[6] The passive form of the word *mashiah* also suggests that God is the agent of this appointment.[7] Therefore, the expression "anointed" implied "the Lord's anointed" *meshiah YHWH* (1 Sam 24:6, etc.), or "the anointed of the God of Israel" (2 Sam 23:2), or referring to God "His anointed" (1 Sam 2:10, Ps 2:2, etc.), "My anointed" (1 Sam 2:35), and the divine presence was usually implied to enable the anointed one to fulfill his mission in his capacity as messiah. Thus it is said in connection to King David's anointing that "the Spirit of the Lord came upon David from that day forward" (1 Sam 16:13; cf. 1 Sam 10:6). The "messiah" was, therefore, within the people of Israel the living sign of God's presence and the constant reminder of the divine promise.

But there is more. The biblical usage of the word "messiah" takes us beyond the local and temporal situation of ancient Israel in the context of the ancient Near East; it speaks about hope in universal terms. Indeed, out of the 39 occurrences of

---

6. James H. Charlesworth, *The Messiah, Developments in Earliest Judaism and Christian Origins* (Minneapolis, MN: Fortress, 1992), xv.

7. On the idea of the "divine passive, " see Christian Macholz, "Das 'Passivum divinum,' seine Anfänge im Alten Testament und der 'Hofstil,'" *Zeitschrift für die neutestamentliche Wissensehaft und die Kunde der älteren Kirche* 81 (1990): esp. 248.

the word "messiah," 30 concern a king; 15 of the 30 refer to David or a Davidic king; and 9 of those apply to the ideal universal king who will come in the future to save Israel and the world.[8] The word "messiah" is, then, loaded with the idea of hope and cosmic redemption. Yet, when the Bible speaks about this ultimate redemption, it does not always mention the word "messiah." Besides, the messianic figure is also represented by other titles or images, such as "seed," "star," or "servant," instead of the explicit term "messiah." Many biblical passages may, then, be "messianic prophecies" and clearly refer to the Messiah without actually using that very word.

A number of testimonies and criteria are, therefore, necessary to determine and establish the quality of "messianic prophecy":

1. Internal evidence from the testimony of the biblical text itself: this implies a thorough exegesis of the text and the search for all the elements and clues suggesting or attesting to the messianic intention.

2. Intertextual evidence from the testimony of biblical tradition as attested in the Hebrew Bible: this implies the search of other biblical texts recognizing our sample text as messianic and thus confirming its messianic character and illuminating its meaning.

3. External evidence from the testimony of extra-biblical tradition: this implies the gathering of classic texts from

8. See 1 Sam 2:10, 35; Pss 2:2; 20:6; 28:8; 84:9; Hab 3:13; Dan 9:25, 26; cf. Walter C. Kaiser, Jr., *The Messiah in the Old Testament* (Grand Rapids, MI: Zondervan, 1995), 16. For a survey on the history of messianism in late antiquity, see Craig A. Evans, "Messianic Hopes and Messianic Figures in Late Antiquity," *Journal of Greco-Roman Christianity and Judaism* 3 (2006): 9–40.

Jewish tradition (Qumran, Talmud, Midrash, etc.) as well as from Christian tradition (the New Testament) interpreting our text as messianic.

The point of contention is not so much, however, the question of how to identify a messianic prophecy. It is quite significant that Jewish and Christian traditions agree on the identification of virtually all messianic prophecies. The crucial problem, indeed, concerns rather the exegetical validity of the messianic interpretation, whether this interpretation can be seriously supported on exegetical grounds.

The challenge and the contribution of this study is to grapple with this exegetical question. The messianic passages, therefore, will be studied from the standpoint of biblical exegesis, taking the Hebrew text seriously, searching for its messianic intention—an enterprise which has rarely, if ever been engaged. For either we contented ourselves with tradition or the testimony of the New Testament, or dismissed altogether the need and even the value of this enquiry on account of the above reasons and theological/philosophical presuppositions.

We shall first pay close attention to the Hebrew text itself, as it is, the way it presents itself, in its finished state, without engaging in any critical discussion in regard to sources and authorship. For our enquiry is not so much about how the text has emerged as it is about what there is in the text that justifies its traditional reading as messianic. We shall then heed the specific literary and historical contexts provided by the texts, their literary structures, their words, and their syntax in order to track down, as far as possible, their original and intended meaning.

We shall also try to capture the meaning which was given to them by other texts of the Hebrew Scriptures referring or alluding to them, and thus try to discover how these messianic texts were understood within the context of the Hebrew Bible, and if they were already recognized as messianic within that tradition. This approach will then be based on the observation of intended intertextual connections between these texts.[9] In order to establish that there is an intended intertextual connection, we will have to make sure that allusions or references are indeed intended in the parallel texts. Specific echoes, the repetition of the same words, literary similarities, and even unique evidence of objective linguistic links will be searched.[10]

Then the ancient classic texts of traditional Judaism, from the early testimonies of the Qumran texts to the Talmud, the Midrashim, and the Targumim, will be consulted to check whether the messianic interpretation of these biblical texts was also attested there.

Lastly, the New Testament allusions and references to these texts testifying to the messianic interpretation will be mentioned.

To be sure, we cannot cover all the messianic prophecies, nor exhaust their meanings they carry. Yet a fair sample of key messianic passages should suffice to draw the lessons of these messianic prophecies and then evaluate to what extent the

---

9. Our reading of the biblical text will then focus on the signs found in the text itself ("text-oriented intertextuality"). For we are interested in "inner-biblical exegesis," that is how a particular text may have been understood and interpreted by another particular text. For a discussion on intertextual connections in the literary corpus of the Bible, implying a process of "inner-biblical exegesis," though from a diachronic perspective, see Michael Fishbane, *Biblical Interpretation in Ancient Israel* (Oxford: Oxford University Press, 1989), 10–14.

10. Cf. Fishbane, ibid., 287–288.

messianic interpretation was in the line traced by the text itself, and eventually to what extent the Christian application to the Messiah Jesus was, is, exegetically correct. In the perspective of this problematic, these messianic texts have also been intentionally selected around the most controversial issues surrounding the debates over the Messiah: (1) His mission in "The Seed" (Gen 3:15); (2) His nature in "The Star" (Num 24:17); (3) His birth in "The Sign" (Isa 7:14); (4) His suffering and death in "The Servant" (Isa 52:13–53:12); and (5) His calendar in "The Sevens" (Dan 9:24–27).

Whatever the results and the conjectures this exegetical enterprise may generate, the implications they may bring along are extremely important. First, they are of significance in regard to the technical domain of biblical hermeneutics since they touch on the critical problem of the fulfillment of biblical prophecies and, by implication, on the nature of the connection between the so-called Old Testament and the New Testament. Also, they bear on the sensitive question of the historical identification of the Messiah: Has the Messiah already come or is He still to be expected? Lastly, and by implication, they may affect the delicate balance of Jewish-Christian relations; for if Christians were right, Jews are not, and vice versa. What lessons shall we learn from the close reading of these complex and controversial texts? A lesson confirming that we are right and the other is wrong? Or a lesson of tolerance and respect: those who think they know will have to learn from those who they thought did not know? On the way to Emmaus we may well hear something else—the unexpected voice of the Messiah.

CHAPTER I

THE SEED

And I will put enmity between you and the woman,
and between your seed and her seed;
He shall bruise your head, and you shall bruise his heel.
(Gen 3:15)

The first potential candidate for this genre of "messianic prophecy" has been found in the first pages of the Bible. It stands out against the background of the first human experience of hopelessness, perhaps the greatest hopelessness of all. After the Creation stories (Gen 1–2), which describe the perfect state of the original creation out of the Creator's hands, Gen 3 reports the first human failure to respond to God's first and only commandment[1]: "Of every tree of the garden you may freely eat; but of the tree of the knowledge of good and evil you shall not eat" (Gen 2:16–17). Adam and Eve ate that fruit. The biblical text does not elaborate on the meaning of that fruit and of that human gesture. We only know about

---

1. The verb *tsawah* ("to command"), from which is derived the word (*mitswah*, "commandment"), is used here (Gen 2:16). The New King James Version is used for biblical quotations throughout. All translations are the author's unless otherwise indicated.

the dramatic consequence of this disobedience: "In the day that you eat of it you shall surely die" (Gen 2:17). Now that Adam and Eve have disobeyed, they can only expect death and evil. This perspective is immediately confirmed in the following texts which speak of a cursed nature full of "thorns and thistles" (Gen 3:17–18) and of the first human violence and the first death of a human: "Cain rose up against Abel his brother and killed him" (Gen 4:8). Indeed the prophecy is given in a context of cosmic hopelessness: "I will put enmity between you and the woman, and between your seed and her seed; He shall bruise your head, and you shall bruise his heel" (Gen 3:15).

The text sounds like a riddle and contains many elements that are "highly symbolic."[2] It speaks about a mysterious conflict involving unidentified beings: the serpent, the woman, the seed; but it also outlines a future scenario of victory whose meaning remains obscure: the serpent will be crushed. The text is not clear, and its key is not given. The interpretations of Gen 3:15 vary dramatically. Is it an etiology, as has been suggested by most critical scholars, a simple legend that is given to justify our present condition and explain why snakes crawl on their bellies and move in the dust, or why men try to kill snakes, and why snakes try to bite men? Or is to be understood more rationally, on the existential level as a reflection of the narrator's anguish and his hope that one day humankind will overcome the forces of evil? Or is it messianic, as it was believed in the oldest Jewish interpretation of the third century B.C., the Septuagint, the Palestinian targums and possibly the

---

2. Gordon, J. Wenham, *Genesis 1–15*, Word Biblical Commentary, vol. 1 (Waco, TX.: Word Books, 1987), 80.

Targum Onkelos, or even in the early Christian interpretation of the New Testament and defended as early as in the second century by Justin (ca. A.D. 160) and Irenaeus (ca. 180)? In regard to the messianic interpretation, the question that arises is whether these ancient Jewish and Christian interpreters were exegetically correct in their reading. Was the messianic interpretation indeed intended by the author of this text? Or is the messianic interpretation only justified as a rereading in the light of subsequent understanding, a *sensus plenior* that would diverge from and even contradict the original meaning of the text itself?[3] An analysis of the literary moves of the text and then a close attention of its words and its syntax should help us to address these questions and determine the possible directions the text itself is suggesting.

Poetic Analysis

The structure of chap. 3, where this prophecy is located, clearly shows the author's intent in bringing this oracle out as the very center of the story:

A vv. 1–5 Serpent-Woman, God absent: forbiddance to eat from the tree

  B vv. 6–8 Adam-Eve: clothes

    C vv. 9–13 God-Adam-Eve

      D vv. 14–15 God-Serpent: "He . . . "

    C¹ vv. 16–19 God-Eve-Adam

  B¹ vv. 20–21 Adam-Eve: clothes

A¹ vv. 22–24 God alone: forbiddance to eat from the tree

---

3. Wenham, *Genesis 1–15*, 81.

The ideas of the whole passage (Gen 3) are organized according to a "chiastic" structure, a literary device, which was often used in the Bible and in ancient Near Eastern literature.[4] In a chiasmus, a sequence ABC is followed by its reverse CBA, "focusing attention on the central element,"[5] in this instance D (3:14–15). This stylistic observation invites then for a careful reading of this single, small unit D which contains our messianic prophecy.

The thematic structure and the word rhythm of this text suggest two strophes. After an introductory statement (or anacrusis) of three Hebrew words, the first strophe (v. 14) progresses in six lines with an irregular word rhythm[6] (2, 2, 3, 3, 2, 3):

Anacrusis: "Because you have done this" (3 words)

1.   "Cursed you are" (2 words)

1.   "More than all cattle" (2 words)

2.   "And more than every beast of the field" (3 words)

3.   "On your belly you shall go" (3 words)

4.   "And you shall eat dust" (2 words)

5.   "All the days of your life" (3 words)

After an anacrusis of one word, the second strophe (v. 15) progresses in four lines with a regular word rhythm (4, 4, 3, 3):

Anacrusis: "Enmity" (1 word)

---

4. See John W. Welch, ed., *Chiasmus in Antiquity: Structures, Analyses, Exegesis* (Provo, UT: Research Press, 1999, 1981).

5. Wilfred G. E. Watson, *Traditional Techniques in Classical Hebrew Verse*, Journal for the Study of the Old Testament, Suppl. Series 170, ed. David J. A. Clines and Philip R. Davies (Sheffield: Sheffield Academic Press Ltd., 1994), 17.

6. The words are calculated in the Hebrew text.

1. "I will put between you and the woman" (4 words)

2. "Between your seed and her seed" (4 words)

3. "He shall bruise your head" (3 words)

4. "And you shall bruise his heel" (3 words)

The contrast between the two strophes is not only indicated through the change of rhythm, but also through the change of thematic orientation. The first strophe is negative and contains a message of hopelessness which concerns the Serpent. The second strophe is positive and contains a message of victory and hope for humankind. In fact, this is the only positive word of the chapter, a window of light in the dark. All these stylistic features aim at the same purpose: they bring out the importance of our passage and provide along the way a framework and specific clues to orient our walk into the mysterious language of the prophetic oracle.

The Serpent

The first enigma concerns the object of the curse: Why a Serpent? We must first notice that our text does not speak of an ordinary serpent among others. The word "serpent" is definite. The oracle is concerned with "*the* serpent" (3:14; cf. 1–2, 4, 13); the animal is thus individualized. This terminology implies then, that this Serpent is unique and is familiar to us. The writer, along with the reader, is supposed to know what (whom) we are talking about. This Serpent belongs to the universal domain. The language of the curse confirms this first impression. The curse places the serpent over all the animals. The Serpent is more cursed "than all cattle, and more than every beast of the field" (v. 14). The word *all* (*kol*) is here repeated three times (*all* the cattle, *all* beasts of the field, *all* the days). And we know that, in our context, this very word is loaded with universalistic overtones.[7] The way this Serpent is described, within the immediate context, gifted with speech, intelligence, and knowledge, making it even superior over humans, suggests that it is not an ordinary snake. Also, the very fact that this Serpent's life goes beyond the actual seed of the woman, since it is not the seed of the Serpent that opposes the seed of the woman but the Serpent itself, that God Himself is addressing the Serpent indicates that "more is involved than an actual serpent."[8]

In the line of Gen 3:15, Hebrew Scriptures often use the imagery of the Serpent to represent the cosmic enemy of God:

> In that day the Lord with His severe sword, great and strong, will punish Leviathan the fleeing serpent, Leviathan that twisted serpent. (Isa 27:1; cf. Ps 74:13–14)

Along the same line, the late Umberto Cassuto, former professor of Bible at the Hebrew University of Jerusalem, interprets the Serpent of Genesis as "the symbol of evil," "the foe of man."[9]

This picture of the Serpent is paralleled in ancient Near Eastern literature, where the serpent often represents a supernatural power gifted with positive qualities such as

---

7. See Gen 2:1–3, 5–6, 9–11, 13, 16, 19; 3:1.

8. Edward J. Young, *Genesis 3: A Devotional and Expository Study* (London: Bannetr of Truth Trust, 1966), 118.

9. Umberto Cassuto, *A Commentary on the Book of Genesis*, trans. Israel Abrahams, vol. 1 (Jerusalem: Magnes Press, Hebrew University, 1989), 142, 160; cf. Medieval Jewish commentators Ibn Ezra and Sforno in *Miqraot Gdoloth* on Gen 3:1.

immortality, knowledge, and wisdom, as well as negative qualities such as evil, chaos, enmity, and death. In Babylonian mythology, *Tiamat* the serpent, primeval cruel monster, was identified with the principle of "evil" against which the god Marduk is called to fight.[10] In Egyptian mythology, the primeval serpent is described fighting the god of light as an inscription on a tomb at Karna testifies: "the serpent Apophis was the enemy of the sun god Ra."[11] In Ugaritic literature, the god Mot urges the "god of life" Baal to engage in a fight against the evil serpent that represents chaos: "If thou smite Lotan, the serpent *slant*, destroy the serpent Tortuous, *shalyat* of the seven heads."[12] The language that describes the Serpent in the text itself, its biblical and even its ancient Near East contexts, all concur to suggest that this Serpent cannot be a vulgar snake; it transcends the ordinary domain of nature and points to a universal or even supernatural being.

The Subject(s) of the Fight

It is, at first, a fight that involves the Serpent and the woman, or rather their respective seed. Indeed, the phrase "between your seed and her seed," explicates[13] the previous statement "between you and the woman," suggesting that the event of the fight will involve the future. The immediate and plain reading of the text

---

10. James B. Pritchard, ed., *Ancient Near Eastern Texts Relating to the Old Testament*, trans. W. F. Albright et al., 3rd ed. (Princeton, NJ: Princeton University Press, 1969), 61–68, 501–503.

11. Edward Conklin, *Getting Back Into the Garden of Eden* (Lanham, MD: University Press of America, 1998), 49.

12. Ibid., 138.

13. This function is indicated by the epexegetical *waw* ("and") that precedes the second statement (see Bruce K. Waltke and M. O'Connor, *An Introduction to Biblical Hebrew Syntax* (Winona Lake, IN: Eisenbrauns, 1990), 652, 653.

suggests that "the woman" refers to the woman who is present in our context, namely Eve; in this case her seed either represents humankind or at least is included in it. Then the text proceeds and describes the next and final step of the fight, "He shall bruise your head, and you shall bruise his heel." It is not clear, however, who is the subject implied behind the third personal pronoun *he* (in Hebrew, *hu'*). Should this pronoun be understood in a neutral sense, referring to the seed, or in a collective sense, referring to mankind or a people, Israel, for instance, or in a particular sense, referring to a specific person? A number of clues observed in the text or in its immediate context point to a single masculine individual as the subject.

It is, first of all, interesting to note that this pronoun receives a special emphasis in the structure of the paragraph and the syntax of the phrase: it appears as the exact center of the strophe at the very moment when the poetic rhythm shifts from four beats to three. It is the hinge of the passage. Moreover, it is the first word in the phrase and occurs before the Imperfect form of the verb, a word order that is quite unusual. Normally, in the Hebrew phrase, the subject follows the verb, especially if the latter is in an Imperfect form, unless emphasis is intended. This accent is then intentionally put on the third personal pronoun *hu'*, suggesting that a particularly important subject is here implied. In fact, the syntax of the phrase suggests that this third personal pronoun subject traces back to God who is the last subject of a verb. In other words, the "He" subject of "bruise" points back to the "I" (of God) subject of "will put," thus implying that behind the "He" who fights could well be the "I" who puts enmity. This syntactical connection may well hint at the divine character of the subject of the verb "bruise" (*shuf*).

18

The Verb of the Fight

The verb *shuf* resonates twice. The two attacks echo each other in the same word *shuf*: "He shall bruise [*shuf*] your head and you shall bruise [*shuf*] his heel." This play on words suggests that the two attacks belong together. Furthermore, the visual image describing the course of the fight confirms this impression, suggesting that the two lethal aggressions belong to the same operation. The heel is hit, while the head is crushed. In fact the heel is hit because it is the heel, with which the Serpent has been hit. The two deaths are therefore described as simultaneous and dependent on each other. This literary device playing on the words and on the visual image clearly shows the intention to relate the two aggressions. These two actions, though one was a bite and the other a crushing, are identified with each other in one and the same event.

It is also noteworthy that although only the head and the heel are mentioned, each antagonist is affected in the totality of his person. A literal translation of the verse will better express the original intention of the text: "He will bruise you, *yeshufka*, [through] the head and you will bruise him, *teshufennu*, [through] the heel." In other words, the idea behind *shuf* affects ultimately the "you" and the "him" and not just the head or the heel. In Ps 139:11 and Job 9:17, the only two other biblical passages where the word *shuf* is used, also the whole person is affected:

> If I say, "Surely, the darkness shall fall [*shuf*] on me."(Ps 139:11

> He who snatches me [*yeshufeni*] for a hair. (Job 9:17)

19

Whatever the exact meaning of the word *shuf* may be, it is clear that the context here suggests a negative connotation of destruction. A cognate word is found in the Arabic language, *shaffa*, where it applies to a cloud approaching and "skimming over the earth,"[14] with the idea of erasing and making it disappear.

The biblical and extra-biblical usage of the verb *shuf* suggests then that in our text it must also be understood in the negative sense of death and disappearance: "He will make you die or disappear [by] bruising your head and you will make him die or disappear [by] bruising his heel" The killing of the Serpent will cost the life of the one who killed it.

Decoding the text, as it is, and analyzing the data it provides, gives then the following scenario. Against the background of hopelessness, the fall of mankind and the cosmic perspective of death and evil, this biblical text predicts the future salvation of mankind in prophetic terms. According to this text, the redemption of mankind will necessarily imply a fight that will involve someone emerging from the future seed of the woman to fight and overcome the Serpent. The victory over the Serpent will cost, however, the death of this fighter. Although that fighter is not clearly identified, the literary accent put on him and his cosmic role suggests that an extraordinary and an important figure is here intended, perhaps of divine origin. This prophecy remains, however, still an obscure riddle. At this stage, we are still unable to clearly identify the particular individual, the subject of this action, or

---

14. G. R. Driver, "Some Hebrew Verbs, Nouns and Pronouns." *Journal of Theological Studies* 30 (1929), quoted in Leslie C. Allen, *Psalms 101–150*, Word Biblical Commentary, vol. 21 (Waco, TX: Word Books , 1983), 251, note 11c. (319, note 11c in 2002 rev. ed.).

to understand the nature of this redemptive event. We need, therefore, to turn to other biblical texts to explore how this text has been understood within the context of biblical tradition and check from there whether our exegesis and our intuitive interpretations are moving in the right direction.

Genesis 3:15 in the Hebrew Bible

Genesis 4:25

The first biblical text, which refers to our messianic text is found just a few verses later, in Gen 4:25. Indeed the word *'ashit*, "I will put" of Gen 3:15, reappears in the name Seth (in Hebrew *shet*) and also in the very verb from which this name derives, namely *shat* ("appointed"). Moreover, in both passages, this word is associated with the same word "seed" (*zera'*):

I will put [*'ashit*] enmity

between your seed [*zera'*] and her seed [*zera'*]. (Gen 3:15)

She named him Seth [*shet*],

"For God has appointed [*shat*] another seed [*zera'*] for me." (Gen 4:25)

These clear echoes on the same two technical words "put" and "seed," call for a reading of Gen 3:15 in connection with Gen 4:25.

The first lesson from the connection between these two passages concerns the nature of the seed. Since the word "seed" in Gen 4:25 does not carry a corporate meaning and refers

21

instead to a specific individual, Seth, it may be concluded that
the seed in the parallel text of Gen 3:15 could likewise refer to
a specific individual.

The second lesson is that God Himself is personally
connected to that seed. In Gen 4:25, it is God who is the
primary subject of the operation, the One who puts (*shat*)
the seed. Eve might have had that prophetic intuition of the
divine presence associated with the seed when, upon giving
birth for the first time, she identifies God as the direct object
of her conceiving and giving birth, as the following literal
translation suggests:

> She conceived and gave birth [*'et*] Cain, and she
> said, "I have acquired [*'et*] a man, [*'et*] the Lord
> [*'Adonai*]" (Gen 4:1)

The last phrase, "*'et 'Adonai*, 'the Lord,' is very strange."[15]
The Lord is in apposition to "a man," referring to Cain. This
construction implies that "the Lord" is identified with Cain
and gives the impression that the Lord was "acquired" by Eve.
Interpreters have been baffled by this syntax. The particle *'et*
has therefore been discarded by most translations, or repointed,
or simply interpreted differently "with the help of" or "from,"
or "as." Yet the particle *'et* introducing "the Lord" is clearly the
definite object marker, thus indicating that "the Lord" should
be the accusative of the verb "I have acquired," just as "a man"
is introduced with the same particle *'et* and is the accusative of
the verbs "conceive" and "give birth." The two lines display
the following parallelism:

---

15. Wenham, *Genesis 1–15*, 101.

She conceived and gave birth to [*'et*] Cain.

She said "I have acquired [*'et*] a man, [*'et*] the Lord [*Adonai*].

This parallelism clearly supports the interpretation that the Lord is to be understood grammatically as the accusative to the verb "acquire." Now, if we respect the syntax of the Hebrew text we are confronted with the most disturbing theological statement, namely that Eve is referring to the Lord Himself. If, indeed, Eve is alluding to the Lord, while giving birth to Cain, she may well point to the previous text of Gen 3:15, to imply that the messianic seed of Gen 3:15 has something to do with the Lord Himself.

2 Samuel 7:12–13

We find the same configuration in 2 Sam 7:12–13,[16] a text dealing with the Davidic covenant:

> I will set up your seed [*zera'*] after you, who will come from your body, and I will establish his kingdom.

> He [*hu'*] shall build a house for My name, and I will establish the throne of his kingdom forever.

Like in Gen 3:15, we find the same particular syntactical construction: the same third personal pronoun *hu'* stands for the antecedent "seed" (*zera'*) and refers to an individual;

---

16. For Collins, 2 Sam 7:12–13 contains the "clearest syntactic parallel" to Gen 3:15." Jack Collins, "A Syntactical Note (Genesis 3:15): Is the Woman's Seed Singular or Plural?" *Tyndale Bulletin* 48 (1997): 144–145.

in this instance the pronoun clearly refers to David.[17] The pronoun is not just mentioned; it is strongly emphasized. Not only the use of the pronoun is not necessary since the person is already implied in the verbal form of the third person, it also appears before the Imperfect form of the verb, which follows a rare and irregular syntax. This pronoun is the actual subject of the verb that describes the fulfillment of the divine promise. These linguistic links between the two texts suggest that 2 Sam 7:12–13 is alluding to Gen 3:15 and applies this old promise to the "seed" of David. Indeed, the numerous prophetic verb forms (prophetic perfects) which are used in 2 Sam 7:12–16 "suggest that the individual who will become David's royal successor had not yet been born."[18] The personal pronoun of Gen 3:15 must therefore have been understood by the author of 2 Sam 7 as referring to an individual who would be a descendant of David.

---

17. It is also significant that the same word "seed" (*zera'*) is applied by Ps 89 to the same Davidic covenant that is mentioned in 2 Sam 7:12–13 (see Ps 89:4, 29, 36; Heb. 5, 30, 37). It is clear indeed that Ps 89 refers to 2 Sam 7. Both texts deal with the same hope, the future establishment of God's covenant with the seed of David and the prophetic dream of the ideal messianic king (see 2 Sam 7:12–13; cf. Ps 89:4). The two passages share the same basic common concern and key words. Both passages insist on the same idea that this seed will "endure forever." In 2 Sam 7 the term "forever" (*'ad-'olam*) appears seven times (2 Sam 7:13, 16, 24, 25, 26, 29 [2 times]). In Ps 89 the same term "forever" is also used seven times: three times in relation to the "seed" (v. 4 [Heb. 5]; vv. 36 and 37 [Heb. 37 and 38]), three times in relation to mercy (*hesed*) in v. 1 (Heb. 2); v. 2 (Heb. 3); and 28 (Heb. 29) and once in relation to God himself: v. 52 (Heb. 53). The same two words are used to qualify this covenant: the noun "mercy" (*hesed*) in 2 Sam 7:15 (cf. Ps 89, where it is used seven times: 1 [Heb. 2], 2 [Heb. 3], 14 [Heb. 15], 24, [Heb. 25], 28 [Heb. 29], 33 [Heb. 34], 49 [Heb. 50]) and the root "establish" (*kun*) in 2 Sam 7:12, 13, 16, 24, 26 (cf. Ps 89:2 [Heb. 3], 4 [Heb. 5], 14 [Heb. 15], 21 [Heb. 22], 37 [Heb. 38]). The same expression "My [or Your] servant" is applied to David in 2 Sam ten times: 7:5, 8, 19, 20, 21, 25, 26, 27, 28, 29 (cf. Ps 89:3 [Heb. 4], 20 [Heb. 21], 39 [Heb. 40]).

18. Lyle Eslinger, *House of God or House of David: The Rhetoric of 2 Samuel 7*, JSOTSup 164 (Sheffield: JSOT, 1994), 45.

Psalm 110

The messianic interpretation of Gen 3:15 is also attested in Ps110, where the very words of Gen 3:15 are recaptured and directly applied to the Messiah, descendant of David, the Davidic Messiah.

> The Lord said to my Lord, "Sit at My right hand, till
> I make your enemies your footstool." (Ps 110:1)

The words of the Psalm (110:1) "Till I make your enemies" (*'ashit 'oybeyka)* are indeed a verbal repetition of the first words of the Genesis promise "I will put enmity (*'eyba 'ashit*). These are the only two texts in the Bible where the association of these two technical words is used. Moreover, it is also related here to the same imagery of the enemy being treaded under the foot as an expression of that same idea of victory: "Till I make your enemies your footstool" (Ps 110:1). Also the familiar theme of "crushing the head" in Gen 3:15 reappears here, " He shall crush the head on many countries" (Ps 110:6, cf. v. 5).[19]

Lastly, the characteristic interplay between the foot and the head, which illustrates in Gen 3:15 the process of salvation, is alluded to in Ps 110 through the skillful device of an *inclusio*.[20] The Psalm starts with a reference to the "the feet" (v. 1) and concludes with a reference to "the head" (repeated twice, vv. 6 and 7). These numerous parallels between the two passages suggest that the author of Ps 110 was referring

---

19. This literal translation is mine; note that the same Hebrew verb *machats* meaning "crush" "break into pieces" (NKJV note) is used twice.

20. It is interesting that the same *inclusio* and interplay between head and foot is used in Ps 68:21–23 (Heb. 22–24) to describe God's victories over His enemies.

to the prophetic promise of Gen 3:15 and interpreted it in a "messianic" sense. The one who was portrayed in Gen 3:15 as crushing the Serpent is now explicitly identified as the Davidic Messiah. In Ps 110, the work of the Messiah goes even beyond the modest agenda of Gen 3:15. He not only crushes the enemy (v. 1) as the seed of Gen 3:15 does, He is now called to sit on the right hand of God to share His kingship[21] and rule with Him (Ps 110:1–2). He is both king and priest and his scope is universal: "he shall execute kings and he shall judge . . . among the nations (Ps 110:5–6), and his priesthood "according to the order of Melchizedek," a "priest of God Most High, possessor of heaven and earth" (Gen 14:18–22), transcends the limits of Israel and is extended toward eternity, le-'olam (v. 4).

Moreover, the interplay between the Lord and the "anointed" (Messiah) even suggests an intention to identify this Davidic Messiah with the Lord Himself:

> The Lord [*YHWH* reads as *Adonai*] said to my Lord [*Adoni*], "Sit at my right hand." (Ps 110:1)

> The Lord [*Adonai*] is at your right hand. (Ps 110:5)

It is noteworthy that in v. 1 it is the Davidic Messiah who sits at the right of the Lord (*YHWH*), while in v. 5 it is the Lord (*Adonai-YHWH*)[22] who sits at the right of the Davidic

---

21. See Ps 110:2. This evocation of kingship is further reinforced by the immediate association with the "rod of your strength" (v. 2), which may designate the scepter (see Ezek 19:14).

22. Several manuscripts and the Targum have here *YHWH* instead of Adonai, see *Biblia Hebraica Stuttgartensia*, ed. K. Elliger and W. Rudolph (Stuttgart: Deutsche Bibelgesellschaft, 1983), ad loc.

Messiah. This play on the relative positions of the Lord and the Messiah is particularly telling. If the one who sits at the right is the Lord, then, the Lord is the Messiah, since the latter is also seen at the right. This kind of visual confusion between the two figures is reinforced by the play between the names of these two figures, *Adoni* (my lord), a word which normally applies to a human person (Gen 33:15), and *Adonai* (the Lord), a name that only applies to God, suggesting again that this *Adoni* is nothing but *Adonai*. This identification is puzzling and disturbs our logic, but the biblical author did not seem to have a problem with this peculiarity.

Summary

The "messianic" interpretation of Gen 3:15 is thus well represented within the Hebrew Bible. The fact that these texts allude or refer to our passage and apply it to a messianic figure allows us, as readers, to do the same. From the exegesis of the text of Gen 3:15 and from its interpretation within the Hebrew Bible, we may, then, infer a number of specific lessons regarding the identity and the function of the messianic figure:

1. In Gen 3:15, the pronoun of the third person, *hu'* was identified as a particular individual of supernatural dimension hinting at God Himself. This divine identification was confirmed by the parallel texts, Gen 4:25, 2 Sam 7:12–13, and Ps 110. He is also identified as a Davidic Messiah by 2 Sam 7 and Ps 110. The particular connection between Gen 3:15 and these texts, which almost function like its commentaries, suggests that the Messianic figure in view

transcends a mere human local king and aims beyond King David at a supernatural being with a cosmic dimension.[23]

2. The same observation holds when it applies to the function of this supernatural being. According to Gen 3:15, He is involved in a cosmic fight which will end with His victory over the serpent representing cosmic evil. On the other hand, according to 2 Sam 7 and Ps 110, He will reign as a universal king who will rule and judge among the nations, but also be "a priest for ever" (Ps 110:4).

Genesis 3:15 in Jewish Tradition

The messianic understanding of Gen 3:15 is also attested in Jewish tradition.

The Septuagint

The messianic interpretation of Gen 3:15 has been preserved in the oldest Jewish interpretations; it is already found in the ancient Greek translation of the Bible, the Septuagint (third century B.C.E.). The translators of the Septuagint did indeed something quite unusual in their rendering of the pronoun: they translated the Hebrew pronoun *hu'* by the Greek pronoun *autos*:

> And I will put enmity between thee and the woman
> and between thy seed and her seed, he [*autos*] shall
> watch against thy head, and thou shall watch against
> his heel.[24]

---

23. Against John J. Collins, who interprets these "messianic" features as a trace of Egyptian influence, see "Pre-Christian Jewish Messianism: An Overview" in Magnus Zetterholm, ed., *The Messiah in Early Judaism and Christianity* (Minneapolis, MN: Fortress Press, 2007), 2–3.

24. In the Septuagint, it is v. 15 in the Greek text, but v. 16 in its English translation (*The Septuagint with Apocrypha: Greek and English*, trans. Sir Lancelot C. L. Brenton [Peabody, MA: Hendrickson Publishers, 1992]).

Out of the 103 passages where the Hebrew pronoun *hu'* ("he" or "it") is translated in the Septuagint, Gen 3:15 is the only occurrence where it does not agree with its immediate antecedent. Indeed, the Greek form of the pronoun (*autos*) refers neither to the woman (it is feminine), nor to the Seed (it is neuter), but it is a masculine singular and only refers to a male individual. This syntactical irregularity shows that the translators did not have in mind a corporate entity, an idea that could have been implied if the woman or the seed was implied. The rabbis of the Septuagint meant a specific person, a man in real history. It is also interesting that in the text of 2 Sam 7:12–13, the same personal pronoun *hu'* is also translated by the same Greek pronoun *autos*, referring here to the Davidic Messiah. This correspondence of translations suggests that for the rabbis of the Septuagint the *hu'* of the parallel text Gen 3:15 referred to the Davidic Messiah. It is also noteworthy that the Septuagint version of Ps 110 (109 in Greek) recognizes the Messiah in this Psalm, since they translate: "I [God] have begotten you before the morning star (*eosphoros*)" (the Hebrew has "from dawn"), possibly an expression for "before the world began" (cf. Prov 8:23), thus alluding to the supernatural pre-existence of this Davidic figure.[25]

The Palestinian Targum

The messianic interpretation of Gen 3:15 is actually recorded in the Palestinian Targum (first century C.E.), which takes the Serpent of Gen 3:15 as a symbol of the Devil who

---

25. See J. Shaper, *Eschatology in the Greek Psalter*, Wissenschaftliche Untersuchungen zum Alten und Neuen Testament 76 (Tübingen: Mohr Siebeck, 1995), 102.; cf. Collins, 18.

will ultimately be overcome at the end of the times by the "King Messiah":

> (Vs. 15) And I will put enmity between thee and the woman, and between the seed of your offspring and the seed of her offspring; and it shall be that when the offspring of the woman keep the commandments of the Law, they will aim right [at you] and they will smite you on the head; but when they abandon the commandments of the Law, you will aim right [at them], and you will wound them in the heel. However, for them there will be a remedy, but for you there will be none, and in the future they will make peace with the heel in the days of the king, Messiah.[26]

Bereshit Rabbah

Likewise the ancient rabbinic commentary to the book of Genesis, the Midrash of Bereshit Rabbah, applies this text to the coming of the Messiah.[27] Commenting on the phrase "all the days of your life" (Gen 3:14), the old Midrash concludes that the struggling against the Serpent "will last until the days of the Messiah." The rabbis of Bereshit Rabbah had affirmed the same hope a few lines earlier:

> R. Berekiah said in the name of R. Samuel b. Nathan: "though these things were created in their fullness, yet when Adam sinned they were spoiled, and they

---

26. John Bowker, trans., *The Targums and Rabbinic Literature: An Introduction to Jewish Interpretations of Scripture* (London: Cambridge University Press, 1969), 122. For the Hebrew version, see Ernest G. Clarke et al., *Targum Pseudo-Jonathan of the Pentateuch: Text and Concordance* (Hoboken, NJ: Ktav, 1984), 4.

27. *Ber. R.* XX, 9.

will not again return to their perfection until the Son of Perez (the Davidic Messiah) comes."[28]

The messianic application of Gen 3:15 is thus well attested in some of the most important and representative sources of Jewish tradition, carrying significant messianic highlights of the biblical interpretation of this passage: the Septuagint clearly identifies the fighter as an individual, the Davidic Messiah who will crush the Serpent; while the Targum and the Midrash, although involving the people of Israel, give the last word and ultimate victory to the Davidic Messiah at the end of times. To these classic references one should add the support of popular traditions in Mystical Judaism that associate the Serpent and the Messiah through the midrashic device of gematria. It has indeed been observed that the numerical value of "serpent"(*nachash*), 358, is the same as the one of "Messiah (*mashiach*).[29] Although this last observation cannot be taken as a strong and serious exegetical evidence, it testifies at least to the memory of an old association of thought relating between the Messiah and the Serpent, pointing to the text of Gen 3:15.

Parallel Texts Recognized as Messianic in Jewish Tradition

The "seed" of **Gen 4:25** is interpreted as a reference to the Messiah:

She called him Seth, for she said, "God has given [*shet*] me another posterity," which means, as R.

28. *Ber. R.* XII, 6.
29. See Charles Ponce, *Kabbalah, An Introduction and Illumination for the World Today* (San Francisco, CA: Straight Arrow Books, 1973), 170, 171.

Tanhuma observed in the name of R. Samuel: "Eve saw the seed which comes from another place, and what is it? It is the King Messiah." (*Bereshit Rabbah 23:7*)

The "seed" of **2 Sam 7** is interpreted by Qumran as the Davidic Messiah who will save Israel:

> "And the Lord declares to you that he will build you a house. And I will raise up your seed after you, and I will establish the throne of his kingdom forever. I will be his father, and he will be my son": he is the Branch of David who will stand with the Interpreter of the Law, who will rule in Zion in the latter days . . . He is the Branch of David . . . who shall arise to save Israel. (*4QFlor (4Q174) f1–2i, 10–13*)

The Lord of **Ps 110:1** is identified as the Messiah:

> R. Yudan said in the name of R. Hama: "In the time-to-come, when the Holy One, blessed be He, seats the Lord Messiah at His right hand, as it is said, "The Lord said unto my Lord: 'Sit thou at my right hand'" (*Midrash Tehilim on Ps. 110:1*)

Genesis 3:15 in the New Testament

In the New Testament, there are a number of texts that have been suspected as alluding in one way or another to Gen3:15.

Galatians 3:16 refers to "the seed, who is the Messiah." **Hebrews 2:14** explains the sacrifice of Christ in terms that remind us of the process described in Gen 3:15, "through death he might destroy him who had the power of death, that is the devil." **Revelation 12:11** speaks of the great Serpent which has also been overcome through the death of the fighter, "by the blood of the Lamb."

But **Rom 16:20** is by far the most explicit allusion to Gen 3:15. In the conclusion of his letter to the Jewish Christians who lived in Rome, the Apostle Paul used Gen 3:15 as a motto of victorious hope:

> The God of peace will crush Satan under your feet shortly.
>
> The grace of our Lord Jesus Christ be with you. Amen.

Paul uses the same imagery and the same motifs of "crushing" and "feet" as in Gen 3:15. It is also significant that Paul's allusion to the text of Gen 3:15 follows immediately his evocation of the human struggle with evil (Rom 16:19). Following the tradition already perceived in the Hebrew Scriptures, Paul identifies the subject, corresponding to the "He" behind the seed of Gen 3:15, as God Himself: "God . . . will crush." Also the event belongs to the future, "shortly." Yet the crushing operation takes place "under your feet," suggesting that although God is the fighter, the beneficiary of the victory is human. God's crushing is interpreted as an act of divine grace on our behalf. It is not an accident that the word "grace" is used in the next line, even identifying the subject of this grace as the Messiah Himself: "the grace of our Lord the Messiah." Paul turns then his slogan of hope into a prayer calling this grace into the flesh of human existence, "be with you. Amen." Hope has now become an inherent part of the present life and has an existential application, supporting our daily struggle against evil.

Just as in Jewish tradition the New Testament attests to the same messianic interpretation for the parallel texts of Gen 3:15. The two texts of 2 Sam 7 and Ps 110 are referred to and directly applied to the Messiah in **Heb 1:1–5**:

> God . . . has in these last days spoken to us by His Son, whom He has appointed heir of all things, through whom also He made the worlds. . . . when He had by Himself purged our sins, sat down at the right hand of the Majesty on high [Ps 110:1; cf. Mark 12:35–37], having become so much better than the angels, . . . For to which of the angels did He ever say: . . . "I will be to Him a Father, and He will be to Me a Son [2 Sam 7:14]?"

The Messianic Fight

An old Jewish legend tells us that the Messiah and the Serpent used to wrestle against each other grasping at each other tightly, rolling in the dust together; and the wrestling was so fierce and so passionate that in the heat of the fight no one could say who was who anymore. This explains, comments the Midrash, why the words "Messiah" and "serpent" have the same numerical value. The confusion is tragic and even frightening. Does it mean that the Messiah has lost His identity? Does it mean that in the course of the battle He has identified with the evil He was supposed to fight and destroy? Does it mean that the Messiah and the Serpent have become the same person and united like twin brothers in a mission against the world? These questions are all the more disturbing as they irrupt in the heart of despair, when all presages the obscure horizon.

Indeed the text of Genesis had warned us that the prospect of death was unavoidable (Gen 2:17). Adam and Eve had just turned down God's invitation to choose life, and therefore the earth and its inhabitants were now under the curse of dust:

> Cursed is the ground . . . dust you are and dust you
> shall return. (Gen 3:17)

Ecclesiastes echoes this text as he meditates on human destiny:

> As he came from his mother's womb, naked he shall
> return, to go as he came; he shall take nothing from
> his labor which he may carry in his hand. (Eccl 5:14)

Since then all humans return to dust, and in funerals at the tombs we all throw the shovel full of dust, in a dramatic gesture to signify our common horizon of dust. There is no hope.

It is against this perspective of hopelessness that the parable of the fight between the Seed and the Serpent outlines a strange scenario of hope. To rescue us from the dust, God Himself will take our place in the dust of the fight. This message is already traced in the very syntax of Gen 3:15 where the struggling seed representing humankind (Gen 3:15a) has been replaced by the "He," (Gen 3:15b) pointing to the great Other, who will, then, hit the Serpent at his head. The confusion between the Messiah and the Serpent reappears between God and humankind. As if God had entered the human realm and identified with the human struggle. The messianic confusion is the whole lesson of Gens 3:15. Behind the "seed," God will fight for us and roll in the dust at our place.

The lesson of Gen 3:15 provides, then, from the first steps of human history with the key for the tragedy of the human condition: unless God comes down and conducts the operation of salvation, unless God fights for us, victory over evil and the dust of death will not be achieved. This particular lesson is carried throughout the Hebrew Scriptures and constitutes in fact the fundamental message of the Bible:

> Do not be afraid. Stand still, and see the salvation of the Lord, which He will accomplish for you today. **The Lord will fight for you**. (Exod 14:13–14)

> Do not be terrified, or afraid of them. **The Lord your God, . . . He will fight for you.** (Deut 1:30)

> You must not fear them, for the **Lord your God Himself fights for you.** (Deut 3:22)

> Our **God will fight** for us. (Neh 4:20)

We perceive the same scenario in the Levitical sacrifice, where the animal takes the place of the sinner and even dies for his sake[30]:

---

30. To be sure the sacrificial system had other applications ranging from the need to express devotion and adoration (Lev 22:17–19) to the wish to signify gratefulness (Lev 7:11–18). Also the various theories of sacrifice have not been exhausted nor have they made justice to the richness and the profound significance of the levitical sacrifices (on these theories, see James G. Williams, *The Bible, Violence and the Sacred, Liberation from the Myth of Sanctioned Violence* [New York: HarperCollins, 1991], 14–20).

> If a person sins . . . he shall bring his trespass offering to the Lord for his sin which he has sinned. . . . The priest shall make atonement for him in any of these matters; and it shall be forgiven him. (Lev 5:1–13)

> If a person commits a trespass, and sins unintentionally . . . he shall bring to the Lord as his trespass offering a ram without blemish from the flocks . . . So the priest shall make atonement for him with the ram of the trespass offering, and it shall be forgiven him. (Lev 5:14–16)

The Hebrew Bible does not explain the historical or theological reasons for this mysterious process. It is simply asserted as a "legal" necessity. The animal sacrifice resonates, then, with the same lesson that is implied in the fight between the "He" behind the seed and the Serpent: the redemption of humankind should be achieved through the process of a sacrifice. To gain the victory against the enemy, the fighter will have to sacrifice himself.

This mechanism of hope did not just apply to the universal history of humankind, or to the national history of Israel, or to the religious community in the cult. This is also the essential principle that governs the life of the one who walks with God, the existential experience that is already at work and verified in the personal journey here and now. The Psalms are all about this cry of faith:

> Why are you cast down, O my soul? And why are you disquieted within me?

> Hope in God. (Ps 42:11)

> Truly my soul silently waits for God; from Him comes my salvation. (Ps 62:1)

The message of faith that carries the whole Bible is indeed anticipated in the lesson of Gen 3:15. Behind the "seed," God will be fighting for us, taking our place in the fire. God's fight, not ours, will lead to victory. The fight against the Serpent, against sin and evil, against death and dust is not my fight. God's fight is then given from the very beginning of human history, as the only solution, the only hope for humankind to overcome the Serpent.

The very fact that this enemy is represented by a serpent, whose characteristic feature is precisely to crawl on its belly, and eat dust, already suggests the fateful defeat of this enemy. This particular imagery borrowed from military language is indeed often used in the Bible to express the idea of victory over the enemy:

> Those who dwell in the wilderness will bow before him.
>
> And his enemies will lick the dust. (Ps 72:9)
>
> The nations shall . . . be ashamed of all their might;
> . . .
>
> They shall lick the dust like a serpent;
>
> They shall crawl from their holes like snakes of the earth. (Mic 7:16–17)
>
> Kings . . . shall bow down to you with their faces to the earth,
>
> and lick up the dust of your feet. (Isa 49:23)

The eating of the dust by the Serpent in Gen 3:15 means, then, victory over the Serpent, and is therefore of great significance.

It is indeed interesting that this "eating of dust" by the Serpent responds to Gen 2:17, which speaks of the "eating" of the forbidden fruit by Adam and Eve associated to the prospect of death; just as it responds to Gen 3:17–19, which speaks of the "eating" from the cursed ground by humans, associated to their fatal return to "dust." Could it be that the divine curse against the Serpent recorded in Gen 3:15 would contain the response to the divine curse against humans? Could it be that beyond the dead end of the curse and the darkness of the night, the wrestling Messiah of Gen 3:15 would give us from the dust where He rolls at our place a glimpse at the morning star?

CHAPTER II

THE STAR

I see Him, but not now;
I behold Him, but not near;
A Star shall come out of Jacob;
A Scepter shall rise out of Israel,
And batter the brow of Moab
And destroy the sons of tumult.
(Num 24:17)

The next sample text takes us into the context of the Israelites final journey in the wilderness as they are approaching Canaan. For the third time, after Sinai and Kadesh, the people of Israel encamp at the foot of a mountain. In many points, the present situation is a reminder of their earlier stopping places. In Sinai, as well as in Kadesh, the revelation was also followed by the story of complaints and the rebellion of the people against God. And as a result, each time the survival of Israel was threatened (Num 14:11–12; 21:46). These parallels suggest again the same prospect of tragedy on the horizon of the third station (see Num 25). And, indeed, Balak the king of Moab has just called his prophet Balaam to curse Israel so that he may be "able to defeat them and drive them out of the land" (Num 22:6).

The prophecy, once again, emerges within the perspective of hopelessness, in the expectation of a tragic event, Israel's harlotry and the plague that follows (Num 25) and under the preparation of a curse (Num 22). The words of the prophet are full of metaphors and sound like a riddle concerning the far future: "I see Him, but not now; I behold Him, but not near" (Num 24:17). The same questions confront again the reader regarding whether this text could qualify as a messianic prophecy. Do these prophetic words and the prophetic scenario apply to an immediate future of the particular history of Israel or to an eschatological future of the universal history of humankind? Who is this ruler here represented by the "star" coming from Jacob/Israel, is He an Israelite king, Saul, David, as proposed by most critical scholars, or a supernatural figure of messianic dimensions? In other words, is this text to be interpreted as a messianic prophecy? Is the original intent of the text messianic, and hence to be interpreted literally and exclusively to refer to an eschatological Messiah? Or is this text just an example of the fuller sense which is only discovered gradually through the meditation of successive generations? Or is this text a *vaticinium ex eventu* prophecy from the time of an Israelite king? To respond to these questions, it is necessary to analyze the text as it is in its context, pay attention to its literary form and its poetic expression and pursue as far as possible the intended meaning of its message, what the biblical author originally meant to say.

Poetic Analysis

The delimitations of Balaam's oracles are clearly indicated through an inclusio. Beginning and end echo each other. The unit begins when the prophet responds to Balak's invitation in Num 22:21: "So Balaam rose [*wayyaqom*] . . . and went [*wayyelek*]," and ends when Balaam leaves the place where he was cursing/blessing in Num 24:25: "Then Balaam rose [*wayyaqom*] . . . and went [*wayyelek*]."

Balaam's prophecy is divided into seven oracles regularly introduced by the same expression, "And he took up his oracle and said," and according to the following structure:

Oracle I. Blessing 1: For Israel (Num 23:7–10)

Oracle II. Blessing 2: For Israel (Num 23:18–24)

Oracle III. Blessing 3: For Israel (Num 24:39)

Oracle IV: A Star from Jacob/Israel (Num 24:17–19)

Oracle V. Curse 1: Against Amalek (Num 24:20)

Oracle VI. Curse 2: Against Kain (Num 24:21)

Oracle VII. Curse 3: Against Asshur, Eber, Amalek (Num 24:23–24)

The first three oracles are blessings that concern Israel (23:7, 24:10). The last three oracles are curses that concern the nations (24:20–24). The contrast between these two series is striking: the blessings on Israel/Jacob are long (18 verses), well-elaborated, full of life (23:10, 22, 24; 24:59), and use many metaphors to express the ideas of vitality and strength (dust, ox, lion); whereas the curses on the nations are short (5 verses), with constant references to death (24:20, 22–24), without any metaphoric language.

The fourth oracle is situated precisely in the middle of the seven oracles. This centrality is furthermore confirmed by the way this oracle is connected to the preceding and the following oracles. On one hand, the first section of the fourth oracle (24:15–16) marks the end and the climax of the blessings; the progression describes Balaam's prophetic response to God's inspiration: from his embarrassed interrogation in "How shall I curse?" (23:8) to affirmation of his intense vision (24:15–16). On the other hand, the last section of the fourth oracle (24:17b–19) introduces and prepares for the curses against the nations, which will follow. The intention of this centrality of this prophecy suggests that it is the most important vision of Balaam's seven oracles.

The Literary Structure of Numbers 24:15–19

The oracle is divided into three parts:

I. Prophetic inspiration (vv. 15–16)
    utterance of Balaam
    utterance of the man whose eyes are opened
    utterance of him who hears, who knows, who sees

II. The vision of the Star (v. 17)
    in time: I see Him, I behold Him, but not now
    in space: a Star out of Jacob, a Scepter out of Israel

III. Destruction of the nations (vv. 17–19)
    Moab
    Edom

44

Prophetic Inspiration

What is striking from the outset is the prophet's awareness of the extraordinary acuteness of his vision. Twice, in the third oracle (24:3–4) and now in the fourth, he stresses his prophetic lucidity. In addition to his ability to hear, which he mentions only once in each passage, he hammers three times the idea of seeing, describing himself as a "man whose eyes are opened . . . who sees the vision of the Almighty . . . with eyes opened wide" (Num 24:3–4, 15–16).

In the fourth oracle, however, another dimension is added to the perception of his senses: the knowledge of the Most High (24:16). Significantly, this additional information is given in the middle of all the other motifs, which are organized in a chiastic manner, according to the following:

A Eyes opened
> B Hears the words of God (*El*)
> > C Knows the knowledge of the Most High
> B¹ Sees the vision of the Almighty (*Shaddai*)
A¹ Eyes opened wide

The structure of Balaam's vision places the knowledge of the Most High at its heart, a way to suggest the supernatural nature of the prophet's inspiration.

A Promise for the Future

The first information of the prophetic word is that it concerns a vision about the future. The Hebrew phrase *'acharit ha-yyamim* "in the latter days" (24:14) is a special expression, which refers to the future and, depending upon its context, can be used in relation to the eschatological time of the coming of the Messiah and of the Kingdom of God (Dan 2:28; 10:14; Ezek 38:16).[1] In fact, the prophet's emphasis on his prophetic ability "to see" confirms the impression that he intends to predict the far future. Significantly, the "I see" which starts the messianic vision (24:17), and echoes the preceding accent on seeing (24:16) opens to the far future: "I see Him, but not now; I behold Him, but not near" (Num 24:17). The reference to the "end" (Num 23:10), the repetition of the idea "but not now," "but not near," confirms that the latter days applies, indeed, to the most distant future, that will end human history. Furthermore, the imagery adds to this eschatological intention.

The metaphor of the "Star" (*kochab*) reminds of Gods promise to Abraham to make his seed "as the stars of the heaven" (Gen 15:5; 22:17). The reference to the "Star" evokes, therefore, the far future when, finally, the divine promise will be fulfilled, and Israel will be like the stars (1 Chr 27:23).

The mention of the "Scepter" is another way to suggest that the event of Balaam's vision belongs to the future. So far, Israel has had no king; only later, after the time of the Judges will Israel be ruled by kings. Speaking about the coming of a king (see also Num 24:7 and 23:21), now when Israel is not yet a kingdom, implies that the prophet does refer to a future situation. This special emphasis on the future of the prophetic vision and on its supernatural nature serves one purpose: to prepare us for the extraordinary figure that is the object of this vision.

---

1. See H. Seebass, "*'acharit*," *Theological Dictionary of the Old Testament*, ed. G. Johannes Botterweck and Helmer Ringgren (Grand Rapids, MI: Eerdmans, 1974), 1:211; cf. Gerhard Pfandl, *The Time of the End in the Book of Daniel*, Adventist Theological Society Dissertation Series, vol.1 (Berrien Springs, MI: Adventist Theological Society Publications, 1992), 178.

The image of the star does not just concern the idea of a divine promise for the future destiny of the people of Israel; in our context, the metaphor of the star seems to fill another function than just representing the people of Israel. In fact, the people of Israel are represented in Balaam's first oracle as "the dust of Jacob" (Num 23:10). Saying that "a Star shall come out of Jacob," which has just been represented by the dust, is suggesting the uncommon nature of this ruler who emerges from Jacob and yet belongs to another order. This identification is further confirmed by the fact that the metaphor of the star is also used to represent heavenly beings and supernatural powers (Dan 8:10; Job 38:7; Isa 14:13; Amos 5:26). It is also noteworthy that in the two other biblical occurrences where a "star" in singular is implied, it always connotes a reference to the superhuman and the divine order (Isa 14:12–13; Amos 5:26).

This direction of thinking is also confirmed by another passage, Num 23:21, which is found in the immediate context of Balaam's prophecy, and which echoes our text:

He has not observed iniquity in Jacob	I see Him but not now
He has not seen wickedness in Israel	I behold Him, but not near
The Lord his God is with him	A star shall come out of Jacob
And the shout of a King is among them	A scepter shall rise out of Israel
(Num 23:21)	(Num 24:17)

47

The two passages display a number of parallels and share a number of common words or synonyms. The same sequence, Jacob and Israel; the same verb "see" *(ra'ah)*, or its synonyms, "observe," "behold" in corresponding places; the repetition twice of the negation *lo'* in connection to those verbs, also in corresponding places; the same reference to kingship in corresponding places (king//scepter). All these correspondences of words and of structure suggest that the line, "a star shall come out of Jacob" corresponds to the line, "The Lord his God is with him [*'immo*]." The mention of the star parallels, then, the reference to God Himself. Note also, that this last phrase is itself in parallel to "the shout of a King is among them [*bo*]"[2] (Num 23:21). Just as the star parallels the "scepter" in Num 24:17, the Lord God parallels the king in Num 23:21. Balaam's language is bold. This future ruler is not just a human king coming from the dust of Jacob; he is also a Star whose special connection to the heavenly and the divine order, manifests God's presence among humans.

The Death of the Righteous

It is certainly not an accident that the theme of death appears in connection to "the dust of Jacob" in Num 23:10, while the theme of crushing and victory appears in connection to "the star of Jacob" in Num 24:17. In the Bible, the motif of "dust" conveys the idea of "death,"[3] while on the other hand, the motif of "star" conveys the idea of glory and victory.[4]

---

2. Note the syntactical parallelism between the two prepositions, literally: "with him" (*'immo*) // "in him" (*bo*).

3. See Gen 3:19; 2 Kgs 23:6; Job 10:9; 34:15; Pss 22:15; 90:3; 104:29; Eccl 3:20; 12:9; Dan 12:2, etc.

4. See Judg 5:20; Isa 14:13.

In fact, the two passages of Balaam's oracles echo each other on a number of specific words and motifs (in bold in the texts):

Numbers 23:9–10 (A)   **Numbers 24:17 (B)**

I. From the top of the rocks
    I see him
    And from the hills
    I behold him

I. **I see him** but not now

    I behold him but not
    near

II. Who can count the dust
    of **Jacob**
    Or number the one fourth
    of **Israel**

II. A star shall come
    out of **Jacob**
    A scepter shall rise out
    of **Israel**

III. Let me die the death of
     the righteous

     And let my end be like his

III. And batter the brow
     of Moab

     And destroy the sons
     of tumult

Not only the echoes are verbatim, the same words and the same grammatical forms are used, but they also appear according to the same sequence. Furthermore, the parallels of associations of the verbs "behold" (*shur*) and "see" (*ra'ah*), and of the names Jacob and Israel (as such, without any preposition) are unique within the whole series of Balaam's oracles. Indeed the parallelism between the two passages is too striking not to be intended and significant. This is a clear indication that the two texts (A and B) are pointing to each other and should therefore be read and understood in connection to each other. The observation of relations between the first two sections (I and II) of the two passages A and B suggests that the third sections (III) are also related: the motifs of "death" and "end" in the third section of A are related to the motifs of "crushing"[5] and "destruction" in the third section of B. In A the focus is on the righteous who dies, and in B the focus is on the victory expressed through the crushing of the enemy. Besides the common negative evocation between death and destruction, the connection between these two themes reminds us of the associations of thoughts in Gen 3:15, where the crushing of the serpent was also related to the death of the righteous.

The identity of this righteous is not revealed. It does not seem, however, that the righteous refers to a corporate entity, since the prophet Balaam identifies himself as an individual with this entity, which he also refers to in the third person masculine singular "his": "Let *me* die the death of the righteous, and let *my* end be like *his*" (Num 23:10b). Although the singular of the personal pronoun him is used in another context to refer to the corporate entity "Israel" (Num 23:21, 24), the fact that this entity is here, identified with the individual Balaam, suggests that in this verse, the word "him" refers rather to a singular individual.[6]

It is also interesting to note the repetitive pattern of Jacob, Israel, and God. Indeed, regularly after the mention of Jacob

---

5. In Hebrew we have the verb *machats* ("crush"; see NIV), the same verb that describes the "crushing" of the head of the nations in Ps 110:6.

6. See Philip J. Budd who also recognizes that "the plural is difficult to justify since *kamohu* 'like him' requires a singular antecedent" (*Numbers*, Word Biblical Commentary, vol. 5 [Waco, TX: Word Books, 1984], 254); cf. W. F. Albright who suggests that the *mem* of the Hebrew word *yesharm* "righteous" is "enclitic and not the sign of the plural" ("The Oracles of Balaam," *Journal of Biblical Literature* 63 [1944]: 213, n. 28a); cf. D. N. Friedman who supports this reading and explains that "the effect of the use of this enclitic *mem* was to preserve the case ending (here genitive), which was otherwise lost in the evolution of the language" ("Archaic Forms in Early Hebrew Poetry," *Zeitschrift für die Alttestamentliche Wissenschaft* 72 [1960], 104.

and Israel, Balaam's oracles refer systematically to God[7] (in bold in the text):

Come curse **Jacob** for me,

And come, denounce **Israel**!

How shall I curse whom **God** has not cursed? And how shall I denounce whom **the Lord** has not denounced? (Num 23:8)

For there is no sorcery against **Jacob**

Nor has He seen wickedness in **Israel**

The Lord his **God** is with him. (Num 23:21)

How lovely are your tents, O **Jacob**!

Your dwellings, O **Israel**!

Like aloes planted by **the Lord,**

God brings him out of Egypt. (Num 24:7, 8)

This repetitive pattern contains a significant lesson in regard to the identity of the righteous in Num 23:10, who also follows the mention of Jacob and Israel:

Who can count the dust of **Jacob**

Or number the fourth of **Israel**

Let me die the death of the **righteous** and my end be like **his**!

---

7. The only exception is Num 24:17 where God is already implied in "the star" coming "out of Jacob" (*miya'aqov*) and in the parallel expression the "One" who "out of Jacob (*miya'aqov*) . . . shall have dominion" (Num 24:19).

Could it be that "the righteous" Balaam is referring to has also in this verse something to do with the Lord Himself?[8]

The Crushing of the Head

The prophetic vision describes this divine figure fighting against a cosmic enemy: "He will crush the foreheads of Moab, the skulls[9] of all the sons of Sheth" (Num 24:17 NIV). The expression "sons of Sheth" is not clear. This name refers perhaps to a country that would be related or even equivalent to Moab, "comparable entities, either neighboring peoples or two names for Moab,"[10] as suggested by the parallelism, just as Jacob/Israel and Edom/Seir (Num 24:17–18). This identification of Sheth with Moab is also attested in Jer 48:45 that quotes this passage and places these two entities in synonymic parallelism. One may also understand Sheth, normally rendered Seth in English, as a hint at the third son of Adam, Seth (Gen 5:3), implying then a reference to the ancestor of the whole humankind, since he was supposed to take Abel's place and carry on Adam's line (Gen 4:25); an interpretation that was taken by the Aramaic Targum.[11] Anyhow, the horizon of the vision seems, indeed, to go

---

8. Note that the word *yashar* "righteous" is also used to characterize God (see Deut 32:4; Pss 24:8; 92:16 [Heb. 15]).

9. The NIV translation of "skulls" (from the reading of the Hebrew *qdqd* rather than *qrqr*) is preferable on the basis of the Samaritan version and Jer 48:45 which quotes this passage.

10. Gordon J. Wenham, *Numbers: An Introduction and Commentary*, Tyndale Old Testament Commentaries (Downers Grove, IL: Inter-Varsity Press, 1981), 179.

11. For modern supporters to this interpretation, see George Buchanan Gray, *A Critical and Exegetical Commentary on Numbers*, The International Critical Commentary (Edinburg: T. & T. Clark, 1956), 371, cf. Timothy R. Ashley, *The Book of Numbers*, The New International Commentary on the Old Testament (Grand Rapids, MI: Erdmans, 1993), 501; and Walter C. Kaiser, Jr., *The Messiah in the Old Testament* (Grand Rapids, MI : Zondervan, 1995), 56.

beyond the local situation. Seven nations are counted: Moab (v. 17), Edom (v. 18), Amalek (v. 20), the Kenites (v. 21), Asshur (v. 22), Cyprus[12] (24a), and Eber (v. 24b). The number seven, which is also the number of the oracles, may be a rhetorical device to suggest the mystical idea of totality. The confrontation of the fighter has a universal scope; it covers all the nations (*goyim*; see 24:20).

The association of Edom and Amalek is particularly significant in biblical tradition. Moab is here associated with Edom (Num 24:18); and Amalek appears to be the dominant figure of the cursed nations; he is called "first among the nations" and is mentioned twice in v. 20. Amalek is recorded as one of the grandsons of Esau (Gen 36:12; 1 Chr 1:36), and Amalekite history ends, as it begins, in the land of Edom (1 Chr 4:43). The reference to Amalek in this text, as one finds it very rarely afterwards in the Bible, may also be a clue suggesting the antiquity of that text,[13] which would, then, exclude a Davidic setting and therefore exclude the idea of a *vaticinium ex eventu* prophecy.[14]

Now, the fact that Moab, the present enemy of Israel (Balak), is associated with Edom and Amalek confirms the particular significance of that conflict. Esau, who was identified with Edom (Gen 36:1), was the first enemy of Jacob-Israel, and Amalek was the first to attack Israel (Exod 17:8). These "first" events will be retained forever in Israel's memory. Edom and Amalek will become the archetypes of the enemy of Israel.

---

12. The Hebrew word is *Kittim* (see NIV) which refers to the town of Kition located in Cyprus and is often used to refer to Cyprus itself (Jer 2:10; Ezek 27:6).

13. See Budd, *Numbers*, 270.

14. See Antti Laato, *A Star Is Rising: The Historical Development of the Old Testament Royal Ideology and the Rise of the Jewish Messianic Expectations* (Atlanta, GA : Scholars Press, 1997), 84.

Numbers 24:17 in the Hebrew Bible

Genesis 3:15

Balaam's oracle recalls the promise of Gen 3:15. The same imagery of the "crushing of the head" (Num 24:17) is used as well as the same word "enemy" ('*oyeb*; 24:18). The same scenario connecting the victory over the enemy with the death of the "righteous;" the same mysterious allusion to a divine involvement. This common language and associations of thoughts between the two oracles suggest that the biblical writer had the same messianic figure and the same event in view This connection between Balaam's oracle and Gen 3:15 suggests that the ruler implied in Balaam's prophecy is the same as the one who crushes the serpent in Gen 3:15, with universalistic and divine dimension and does not support, therefore, the critical reading of "another *vaticinium ex eventu* from the time of David (and Solomon)."[15]

Genesis 49:9–12

Balaam's vision shares also a number of common motifs with Gen 49:9–12. Already a few verses earlier, Balaam blesses Israel with the same words and the same imagery as Jacob's blessing of Judah:

> He bows down, he lies down as a lion;
>
> And as a lion, who will rouse him? (Num 24:9)
>
> He bows down, he lies down as a lion;
>
> And as a lion, who shall rouse him? (Gen 49:9)

---

15. Ibid., 84.

In Balaam's oracle, the coming of the future ruler is described in the same language as in Jacob's blessing. In both prophecies, the ruler is viewed as emerging from the people (Jacob/Judah); and in both passages we have the same imagery of the scepter (*shevet*) and the repetition of the same preposition from (*mi*):

> A star shall come out from [*mi*] Jacob;
>
> A scepter [*shevet*] shall rise up from [*mi*] Israel. (Num 24:17)
>
> A scepter [*shevet*] shall not depart from [*mi*] Judah,
>
> Nor a lawgiver from [*mi*] between his feet
>
> Until Shiloh comes and to him shall be the obedience of the peoples. (Gen 49:10)

This parallel of language suggests that the two oracles are referring to the same figure. Jacob's prophetic blessing provides us, however, with a supplement of information regarding this ruler. He is not just coming from Jacob, as Balaam indicates; the scepter is now attributed to Judah, the tribe of the King David. Whatever explanation we give to the mysterious word Shiloh that seems to characterize this ruler[16] in the next line, it remains clear that the text involves a ruler of universal scope, since "peoples,"[17] and not just Israel owes him obedience (see Gen 17:6; Exod 15:16; Deut 32:8).

---

16. A variety of meanings have been proposed for the word *Shilo*, from a place controlled by the ideal Judean king to a person, the Judean ideal king himself, or to a phrase expressing the bringing of the tribute to this ideal Judean king. For a review of these meanings, see Gordon J. Wenham, *Genesis 1–15*, Word Biblical Commentary, vol. 1 (Waco, TX: Word Books, 1987), 477–478.

17. The word "people" is used in the plural *'amim* in the Hebrew text of Gen 49:10.

Furthermore, Gen 49:10 introduces a temporal element: "The scepter shall not depart . . . until." This specification suggests that the whole Judean royal line will reach its ultimate climax with this ruler, thus implying a messianic interpretation to this kingship, a perspective that is confirmed by Zech 9:9–10 reading of this passage; the same association of "king" and "donkey" is indeed used there to describe the ideal Davidic king as a messenger of peace, "just" and "lowly" and having dominion over the whole world, "from sea to sea . . . to the ends of the earth" (Zech 9:10).

Obadiah

The prophecy of Obadiah is clearly constructed on Balaam's oracle against Edom. The two texts, which are both characterized as "prophetic vision" (*hazon*/*hazah*: Obad 1, cf. Num 24:14) and as "oracle" (*ne'um*: Obad 4, cf. Num 24:15), share the same words, phrases, specific expressions, and ideas:

> The Hebrew verb *qum* "rise" to describe the attack against Edom (Obad 1, cf. Num. 24:17.

> The word *yerash* "possession" referring to the victory over Edom is used in both places as a key word (5x in Obad 17, 19, 20 and 2x in Num 24:18).

> The word *serid* "remnant" for the survivors of Edom (Obad 14, 18, cf. Num 24:19).

> The mention of total destruction of the enemy (Obad 14, 16, cf. Num 24:17, 20, 24) and the use of the verb *'abad* "destroy" (Obad. 8, 12; cf. Num 24:19).

56

The word play (3x) on the verb *shatah* "drink" in connection with the expression *kol ha-goyim* "all the nations" in Obad 16 echo the word *shet* Seth in the expression *kol beney shet* all the sons of Seth in Num 24:17.

The reprisal upon the "head" of the enemy in Obad 15 evokes the crushing of the head of the enemy in Num17 (cf. Gen. 3:15).

Edom's self-appointed as a "star" (Obad 4) points to the "star" of Jacob (Num 24:17).

The unique common use of the phrase *sim qinka* "put your nest" (Obad 4; cf. Num 24:21).

As Michael Fishbane concludes after noting some of the parallels between these two biblical passages: "One can hardly doubt that this prophecy was intended to fulfill the ancient prophetic words of Balaam, who predicted the stellar rise of Jacob in Num 24:17."[18] These connections attest, at least, that Obadiah, whose messianic intention has been recognized by a large number of scholars,[19] interpreted Balaam's prophecy in a messianic sense. The judgment of the nations and the universal salvation and that which Balaam saw is again proclaimed by Obadiah (Obad 2021, cf. Num 24:19, 23). Furthermore, the same eschatological perspective leading to God's universal reign and dominion is even more

---

18. Michael Fishbane, *Biblical Interpretation in Ancient Israel* (Oxford: Clarendon Press, 1989), 478.

19. See Gerard Van Groningen, *Messianic Revelation in the Old Testament* (Grand Rapids, MI: Baker Book, 1990), 461.

explicit in Obadiah's prophecy that concludes with the final promise that "the kingdom shall be the Lord's" (Obad 21). One significant new illumination that Obadiah brings into Balaam's prophecy concerns the identity of the agent of this salvation. While Balaam refers to "the star of Jacob," as the ruler who will crush the forces of Edom, Obadiah speaks of *YHWH* for the same operation:

> "Will I not in that day," says the Lord, "even destroy the wise men from Edom, and understanding of Esau . . . To the end that everyone from the mountains of Esau may be cut off by slaughter." (Obad 8, 9)

For Obadiah the one who will judge and usher the final day is not a royal human person; He is none else but the Lord Himself.[20] In other words, for Obadiah, the Lord *YHWH* plays the role of the ruler seen by Balaam.

Micah 5:2 (Hebrews 5:1)

The text of Mic 5:1 echoes the language of Num 24:17 (and Gen 49:10) to proclaim the emergence of the ideal future ruler of Israel.

Out of [*mi*] you [Bethlehem]

From of [*mi*] old from [*mi*] everlasting. (Mic 5:2; Heb 5:1)

In this passage, the origin of the ruler suggests an unexpected tension. He comes from Bethlehem, "little among the thousands of Judah;" but he also comes "from of old, from everlasting." His Davidic lineage is implied in the reference to the little village of Bethlehem, and his

---

20. See Van Groningen, ibid.

supernatural derivation is implied in the expression "from of old" and "from everlasting." He originates both in time and in eternity. We remember that the same tension was suggested in Num 24:17, where the ruler was identified both as a superhuman being represented by the star and a human king represented by a scepter coming out of Jacob and Israel. This association of the two orders, the divine order and the human order, which are normally emphatically separated in the Bible, are here brought together as a necessary association for the efficiency of the redemptive operation.

Amos 9:11–12

Amos associates the motifs of "possession of Edom," remnant, and victory over all the enemies, as found in Num 24:18, to describe the universal victory of the future Davidic king over all the nations:

> "On that day I will raise up the tabernacle of David, which has fallen down, and repair its damages; I will raise up its ruins, and rebuild it as in the days of old; that they may possess the remnant of Edom, and all the Gentiles who are called by my name." Says the Lord who does this thing. (Amos 9:11–12).

Jeremiah 48:45

Likewise, Jeremiah repeats the same technical language and the same stylistic expression contained in the text of Balaam's oracle in connection to Edom in order to evoke the events, which will take place in the latter days:

"A fire shall come out of Heshbon,
A flame from the midst of Sihon,
and shall devour the brow of Moab, the crown of the
head of the sons of tumult. . . . In the latter days,"
says the Lord. (Jer 48:45–47)

Besides the phonetic, lexical, and thematic commonality
("crush," "head," "Moab," "sons of Seth") with Num 24:17,
one should note the same stylistic parallel of the coming
out of the fire and of the flame and the same use of Hebrew
preposition *mi* ("from"):

A fire shall come out of [*mi*] Heshbon	A star shall come out of [*mi*] Jacob
A flame from the midst of [*mi*] Sihon	A scepter shall rise out of [*mi*] Israel
(Jer 48:45)	(Num 24:17)

We remember that it is the same rhythm and the same style
we noticed in Jacob's blessing in Gen 49:10, announcing the
coming of the Shiloh, thus paralleling the star of Num 24:17
and the fire-flame of Jer 48:45.

Daniel 11:30

In his eschatological vision of wars,[21] anticipating the time
of the end (Dan 11:40–45), Daniel also refers to the threat of
"ships coming from Cyprus" (Heb. *Kittim*) (Dan 11:30, cf.
Num 24:24). The historical application of Daniel's vision is
not clear, but the fact that Daniel uses the same language as

---

21. See Jacques Doukhan, *Secrets of Daniel: Wisdom and Dreams of a Jewish Prince in Exile* (Hagerstown, MD: Review and Herald Publishing Association, 2000), 73–98.

Balaam's oracle in an eschatological perspective shows at least that Balaam's oracle was preserved in Daniel's memory as a prophetic indication for the messianic events.

All these parallels between the texts of the late prophets and Balaam's oracle not only testify to the biblical tradition of the messianic reading of this text, but hint also to the historical fact that these nations were never totally overcome, implying, therefore, another future for this fulfillment.[22] In fact, the defeat of the nations cited in Balaam's oracle as well as the rise of Cyprus, which appear only later on the historical scene, would hardly allow the identification of this king as David, and therefore rather support the possibility of a messianic allusion.

Psalm 110

Balaam's oracle shares a number of verbal parallels with Ps 110. We may note the following:

ne'um "oracle" (Num 24:17, cf. Ps 110:1)

radah "rule" (Num 24:19, cf. Ps 110:2)

machats "crush" (Num 24:17, cf. Ps 110:6)

'oyeb "enemy," with pron. suf. (Num 24:18, cf. Ps 110:2)

Also, the general theme of victory over enemies, as well as the motifs of "scepter" and "heads," are common between the two texts, (Num 24:17, cf. Ps 110:2). These significant echoes between the two passages suggest that Ps 110 is consciously alluding to Balaam's fourth oracle and places Balaam's oracle in its messianic perspective. Also, the fact that this Psalm

---

22. See Wenham, *Numbers*, 183.

refers both to the prophecy of the seed in Gen 3:15 and to the prophecy of the star in Num 24:17, shows the interrelation between the three texts and confirms the messianic tradition associated with them.

Summary

Within the actual context of war and the dark perspective of defeat, as the very survival of Israel is threatened, Balaam's prophecy is a vision of the far future about victory and glory, a vision of hope, which enriched by its parallel texts, provides us with the following information:

1. The messianic portrait reveals a dual nature, divine and human. The Messiah is identified as a star suggesting a supernatural origin, the Lord, God Himself (Num 23:10, cf. Ps 110:1, 5), "whose goings forth have been of old, from everlasting" (Mic 5:2); but He also originates from the dust of Jacob (Num 23:10), and from the "little among the thousands of Judah" (Mic 5:2). The Messiah's line is thus traced from Jacob and Judah explicitly by Balaam, and later from David implicitly by Micah, who sees the Messiah originating from Bethlehem, the city of David (cf. 1 Sam 16:1–13).

2. The Messiah will rule and submit the nations (Gen 49:10; cf. Ps 110:6) and crush all the enemies of Israel and thus ensure peace forever (Gen 49:11; cf. Zech 9:9–10; Ps 110:2, 6). The impact of this Messiah is universal. The horizon of the final battle will embrace the whole earth, all the nations (Num 24:17–24, cf. Gen 3:15). And yet the cosmic destruction of the enemy is associated with the death of the "righteous" (Num 23:10), who could be identified as God, and reminds of the strange scenario projected in Gen 3:15.

Numbers 24:17 in Jewish Tradition

The Septuagint

The text of Balaam's oracle in the Septuagint predicts that "there shall come forth a man from his seed, and he shall be lord over many nations, and his kingdom shall be exalted above Gog" (Num 24:7 LXX). This "man" is then identified as the "star of Jacob:" "A star shall rise out of Jacob; a man shall rise out of Israel" (Num 24:14 LXX). The messianic value of the title of "the man" is well attested in the Septuagint,[23] as we have it, for instance, in Isa 19:20, where the title "the man" appears again to refer to the eschatological savior, "a man who shall save them" (Isa 19:20 LXX). Also, the reading of the name "Gog," instead of "Agag" in Num 24:7,[24] which can only be the Gog of Ezek 38:2, which contains the only other biblical reference to Gog, betrays the intention of the Septuagint to read Balaam's oracle in a messianic sense. The reference to Gog in the book of Ezekiel is, indeed, associated with the eschatological wars preparing for the messianic redemption (Ezek 38–39) and has been identified in rabbinic literature "with the messianic wars preceding the advent of the Messiah."[25]

Qumran

The messianic interpretation of this passage is also found in Qumran literature where it is applied to the Leader of the

---

23. On "the man" as a messianic title, see Miguel Pérez Fernández, *Tradiciones mesiánicas en el Targum Palestinense : estudios exegéticos* (Valencia, Spain: Artes Gráficas Soler,1981), 220–286.

24. This reading is also attested in the Samaritan Pentateuch as well as in Aquila, Symmachus, and Theodotion (see *BHS*).

25. R. J. Werblowsky and Geoffrey Wigoder, *The Oxford Dictionary of the Jewish Religion* (Oxford: Oxford university Press, 1997), 279.

nation, a Davidic war leader who was to arise in the Last Days,[26] and crush all the nations:

> May you trample the nations like mud in the streets!
> For God has established you as the "scepter"
> (Numbers 24:17). (1Q28b, 1QSb)[27]

In another passage the same royal figure from the Davidic line is identified as the "star" of Balaam's oracle:

> The star is the Interpreter of the law, who will come
> to Damascus, as is written: "a star has left Jacob, a
> staff has risen from Israel" (Numbers 24:17). The
> latter is the Leader of the whole nation; when he
> appears, he will "shatter all the sons of Sheth" (Num
> 24:17) (aQ268)[28] "A star moves out of Jacob, and a
> scepter arises out of Israel." The scepter is the prince
> of the whole congregation and when he rises he will
> "destroy all the sons of Seth." (CD 7:19–21)

Targumim

The traditional Aramaic translations of the Pentateuch conveys the same tradition and applies Num 24:17 to the eschatological Messiah who will have dominion "over all mankind."

Targum of Onkelos

> I see him, but not now;
> I observe him, but he is not near;
> A king will emanate from Jacob;

---

26. Michael Wise, Martin Abegg, Jr., and Edward Cook, *The Dead Sea Scrolls, A New Translation* (New York, NY: HarperCollins Publishers, 1996), 149.
27. Quoted in *The Dead Sea Scrolls*, 150.
28. Quoted in *The Dead Sea Scrolls*, 58.

And the Messiah will be anointed from Israel;
He will kill the princes from Moab,
And rule over all mankind.

Targum of Jonathan

I see him, but he is not yet here, I behold, but he is not
here: it is when . . . the Messiah will be consecrated .
. . he will kill all the sons of Seth; the armies of Gog
. . . will fall before him.

The Talmud

The Talmud of Jerusalem witnesses to the same tradition
in connection to Bar Kochba,[29] whose name means the son of
the Star by reference to Balaam's prophecy:

R. Simon B. Yohai taught that his master R. Akiba
used to apply the verse of Numbers 24:17, "a star
will rise from Jacob" to the coming of Bar Koziba,
and Akiba used to say when he saw him: "here is the
Messiah King!" (*J. Taanit* 68b).

Pesiqta Zutarta

The Midrash comments on Balaam's prophecy and
identifies the star as being the Messiah, Son of David:

Numbers 24:17, "I see him:" This is the King
Messiah. "A star shall come out of Jacob." On it our

---

29. The same tradition appears in connection to Alexander Yannai, the
Hasmonean king of Judea and high priest (103–176), who imprinted a star on his
coins as a symbol to suggest that he was to be recognized as the Messiah (See Jacob
Milgrom, *Numbers*, JPS Torah Commentary [Philadelphia, PA: Jewish Publication
Society, 1990], 207).

masters have taught: the Son of David will come . . .
"And a star will come from the East": this is the star
of the Messiah. (*Pesiqta Zutarta* on Num 24:17)

Tanhuma

There, also, the star is the Messiah:

R. Samuel said: "until the day when He will come
the one on whom it is written in Numbers 24:17,
'a star shall come out of Jacob:' this is the King
Messiah." (*Tanhuma* on Deut 2:5)

Bamidbar Rabbah

The Midrash applies Balaam's prophecy to the time of the
end when Israel will be delivered from all their enemies:

One day, in the time of the Messiah, the Israelites
will overcome all the nations, as it is said in Number
24:17, a "star shall come out of Jacob." (*Bamidbar
Rabbah* 2, 12)

Aggadat Mashiah

And a star will sprout out from the east. This is the
star of the Messiah, and it will abide in the east .
. . and if it tarries longer, it will be to the good of
Israel . . . And the Divine voice rings out again:
"Go to Edom, and perform My vengeance!". . . And
instantly King Messiah reveals himself and says to
them: "I am he, King Messiah, for whom you were
waiting!" (*Aggadat Mashiah*, BhM 3:141–144)[30]

---

30. In Raphael Patai, *The Messiah Texts* (Detroit, MI: Wayne State University
Press, 1979), 177.

Parallel Texts Recognized as
Messianic in Jewish Tradition

The Shiloh of **Genesis 49:10** is identified as the Messiah:

> The kings and the rulers will not cease in the house
> of Judah . . . until the coming of the Messiah to
> whom the nations will submit themselves. (*Targum
> of Jonathan* on Genesis 49:10)

> "Until Shiloh comes": this is the King Messiah, to
> whom the nations will obey. *(Bereshit Rabbah* 98, 5)

> Regarding the Messiah, what is his name? Those of
> the school of R. Sheila said: "His name is Shiloh,
> for it is said in Genesis 49:10, 'until Shiloh comes.'"
> (*Sanhedrin* 98b)

The text of **Amos 9:11** is used by the Talmud as a messianic
support:

> R. Nachman says to R. Isaac: "Maybe you heard
> about the time when the son of the fallen will
> come." Then the other asked: "Who is the son of
> the fallen?" He answered: "It is the Messiah." The
> other responded: "You call the Messiah, son of
> the fallen?" The other answered: "Indeed, for it is
> written: 'On that day, I will raise up the tabernacle
> of David, which has fallen down,' Am. 9:11."
> (*Sanhedrin* 96b; cf. *Yalkut Simoni*, Amos 9:7)

On the basis of **Micah 5:2**, Bethlehem is given as the
birthplace of the Messiah:

> The King Messiah was already born . . . from where
> is he? From the royal city of Bethlehem in Judah, as

it is said, "But you, Bethlehem Ephrathah . . ." see Micah 5:1. (*J. Berakhot* 5a)

And you Bethlehem Ephrathah, which is too small to be counted among the thousand of the house of Judah, from you in my name, will come the Messiah. (*Targum of Jonathan* on Micah 5:1)

The messianic application of **Obadiah** by the Midrash Rabbah is particularly interesting as it is brought out in connection to the prophecy of Balaam, thus supporting the tradition of understanding Obadiah as a messianic reading of Balaam's prophecy:

God said: "Wait until the King Messiah comes and fulfill what is written . . ." Jacob said to Esau: "I have still until now to raise the King Messiah, of which it is written, 'a child is born'" (Is. 9:6) . . . Then Israel said to the Holy Blessed Be He [God]: "Lord of the world, how long are we to be subjected to him [Esau/Edom]?" He answered to them: "Until the day comes when 'a star shall come out of Jacob, a scepter shall rise out of Israel'" (Num. 24:17). As soon as the star will come out of Jacob, the stubble of Esau will burn. How can we deduce this? From this text of Obadiah 1:18, which says: "The house of Jacob shall be a fire, and the house of Joseph, a flame; but the house of Esau shall be stubble; they shall kindle them and devour them, and no survivor shall remain of the house of Esau." The Holy Blessed Be He [God] said: "At this hour I will make appear my

kingdom and I will reign upon them, as it is written
in Obadiah 21, 'saviors shall come to mount Zion to
judge the mountains of Zion, and the kingdom shall
be the Lords.'" (*Devarim Rabbah*, Par. 1, Deut. 2:4).

Numbers 24:17 in the New Testament

The New Testament never actually quotes Num 24:17,
but alludes to it in **Matt 2:2** through a number of common
wordings and associations. Here the text tells the story of the
Magi who ask:

Where is He who has been born King of the Jews?
For we have seen His star in the East and have come
to worship Him. (Matt 2:2)

The magi, like Balaam (Num 23:7), come "from the east,"
in Greek *apo anatolon*, which means literally "from its rising"
(of the sun). Significantly, the same Greek verb *anatellein* is
also used in the Septuagint to refer to the "rise" of the messianic
Star in Num 24:17. This play on the word *anatole* suggests
that Matthew made a conscious allusion to Num 23 and 24 on
the basis of the LXX.

It is also interesting, and certainly not a coincidence that
just a few verses before Matthew had mentioned "Immanuel"
that is translated "God with us" (Matt 1:23). The expression is,
indeed, very close to the phrase of Balaam's oracle, "the Lord
his God with him" (Num 23:21). This echo not only confirms
Matthew's allusion to Balaam's prophecy, but also suggests
that he understood the parallel between the star and the "God
with us."

It is also possible that the use of the imagery of the morning star in **2 Pet 1:19** to denote the coming of the Messiah is an allusion to Balaam's oracle. Here again, we find the same Greek verb *anateile* ("rise"):

> We also have the prophetic word made more sure, which you do well to heed as a light that shines in a dark place, until the day dawns and the morning star rises [*anateile*] in your hearts.

It is noteworthy that in our text the two images of the star and the sunrise are closely associated, since the morning star accompanies the first glimmerings of dawn, thus introducing daylight into the world. It is probably this association that led to the interpretation of the star as the morning star, which is found applied to the Messiah in the book of Revelation:

> I, Jesus, have sent My angel to testify to you these things in the churches,
>
> I am the Root and the Offspring of David, the Bright and Morning Star. **(Rev 22:16)**

The Messianic Hope

The ancient rabbis were puzzled by the contradictory representations of the people of Israel. Sometimes the Israelites were compared to dust. Sometimes they were compared to stars. The reason for this difference, they suggested, is that when Israel is wicked they are like the dust, and when they are righteous they are like the stars.[31] This image borrowed

---

31. *Megilah* 16a.

from the biblical texts was not a mere rhetorical way to rebuke the people. Beyond this call for righteousness, through the imagery of the stars in contrast to the dust, hope was then intended. Likewise, Balaam's imagery of the star emerging from the dust of Jacob is a sign of hope.[32]

The same association of the ideas of dust and stars was already heard in the name of Jacob when he wrestled in the dust with the angel. In Gen 32, the Hebrew text plays on the words '*abaq*, which means "to wrestle" or "dust," suggesting the rolling in the dust by the wrestlers and the name of *y'qb*, Jacob[33]:

---

32. It is interesting to note that the star has become an important symbol of hope in Judaism. It has received a pervasive usage in Jewish life, whether religious, liturgical, social, or even political. It appears everywhere in synagogues or even on jewels and in cultic articles (*mezuzoth, siddurim,* etc.) Its name, the magen David ("shield of David"), which has messianic resonances, is heard in the third benediction after the reading of the *Haftarah*, where it designates God Himself. In some mystical circles it referred to the Messiah. But the symbol of the star became particularly widespread in the nineteenth century when the Jews were looking for a symbol that would represent Judaism as the cross did for Christianity. Interestingly and paradoxically, both Judaism and Christianity adopted a messianic symbol to represent themselves. But their messianic symbolism conveyed an essentially different message. While the Christian symbol, the cross, pointed to a human Messiah on the earth and was a sign of death, the Jewish symbol, the star, pointed to a divine Messiah in heaven and was a sign of eternal life. The contrast is too symmetric to be meaningless. It is not surprising that Jewish philosopher Franz Rosenzweig, reflecting on the meaning of the relationship between Judaism and Christianity in his book *The Star of Redemption* (trans. William W. Hallo from 2nd ed. of 1930 [New York: Holt, Rinehart and Winston (1971)]) chose the symbol of the star as an allegorical basis for his theology of Judaism versus Christianity. The symbol of the star became so characteristic of the Jewish identity that the Nazis used it on the identifying badge, the infamous "yellow star" that Jews had to wear throughout Europe. At last, ironically and significantly the star ended up on the Israeli flag. It is again a sign of hope, as if beyond the "here" and "now" of the survivors from the ashes of the Holocaust the star pointed to the "there" of the future.

33. See Gordon I. Wenham, *Genesis 16–50,* Word Biblical Commentary, vol. 2 (Dallas, TX: Word Books, Publisher, 1994), 288.

Then Jacob ['*qb*] was left alone; and a Man wrestled ['*bq*] with him until the breaking of the day. (Gen 32: 24)

It is interesting to notice that Jacob's wrestling experience is associated three times with sunrise:

A Man wrestled with him until **the breaking of the day**. (Gen 32:24)

And He said, Let Me go, for **the day breaks**. (Gen 32:26)

Just as he crossed over Penuel **the sun rose on him**. (Gen 32:31)

The first light of dawn, the flash of the morning star, marked the end and the climax of his wrestling with God in the dust. Balaam describes the same phenomenon of this passing from dust to star. Balaam's first blessing of Jacob refers to dust, "who can count the dust of Jacob" (Num 23:10) and his last blessing refers to the Star, "A Star shall come out of Jacob" (Num 24:17); as if the Star had emerged from and in distinction from the dust. The significant parallel between the two texts, both bringing the star at the end of the dust, suggests that Balaam may also have the morning star in mind.

This imagery is particularly loaded with meaning in ancient Middle Eastern culture, where the stars, and especially the morning star, were worshiped as divine beings.[34] It, first of all, evokes the divine dimension, which belongs to the

34. See R. E. Clements, "*kokhab*," in *Theological Dictionary of the Old Testament*, ed. G. Johannes Botterweck and Helmer Ringgren (Grand Rapids, MI: Eerdmans, 1974), 7:76–77.

heavenly order versus the human dimension, which belongs to the earthly order. As we have already indicated, the biblical image of the Star in the singular expressed the reference to a supernatural Being. In Balaam's oracle the Star of Jacob may well stand for God's presence on Jacob's side, as affirmed in the parallel text, "the Lord God is with him" (Num 23:21).

When the Star appears in connection to the dust, it is to affirm the paradigm of hope: God will not confine Himself in His infinitely distant place; He will move from there and go down here and dust Himself. God will not let the dust remain dust. The Star will come out of dust and bring life out of it. Such wonder of victory over death confirms in itself the necessary presence of the divine Being. For only God the Creator can wrestle in the dust and turn dust into the morning star. Only the God who would come down and dust Himself, "only the God with us" could rescue us from the dust of death The ancient Egyptians conceived the survival of Pharaoh using the same bold image. They believed that after his death the Pharaoh would overcome the chains of dust and take off in heaven and become a star.[35] The book of Daniel uses the same image of the "stars" to describe victory over death:

> And many of those who sleep in the dust of the earth shall awake . . .

---

35. See Pyramid Text 509: "Osiris was embalmed so that he might go forth to the sky among the imperishable stars," in R. O. Faulkner, *Ancient Egyptian Pyramid Texts* (Oxford: Clarendon Press, 1969), 184–185. Cf. also the "Book of the Two Ways" which refers "to afterlife in which deceased commoners become stars in the sky" (L. H. Lesko, "Ancient Egyptian Cosmogonies and Cosmology," in B. E. Shafer, ed., *Religion in Ancient Egypt: Gods, Myths, and Personal Practice* [Ithaca, NY: Cornell University Press, 1991], 102).

Those who are wise shall shine . . . Like the stars
forever and ever. (Dan 12:2, 3)

The coming of the Star out of the dust suggests, then, the
miracle of life out of death; it evokes the wonder of resurrection,
which, as we have seen, may well be implied in Num 23:10,
where Balaam refers to the "death of the righteous."[36]

The image of the Star does not just refer to the messianic
promise of the coming of the Davidic Messiah, anticipating
the new day after the night; it contains with it the promise of
our own survival, as human living beings. The curse of Gen 3,
which condemned humans to dust, will be reversed. Our nature
of dust will change into something else opposite to dust. As
much as dust meant here bellow, stars would mean infinitely
far up there; as much as dust meant darkness and death, stars
would mean light and life. We will not just survive dust.

This cosmic language and hope suggest that these prophetic
words were aiming far beyond the anguished Israel of that time.
What Balaam saw concerned "the latter days" (Num 24:14),
"not now," "not here" (Num 24:17). The target was of universal
scale and was related to the future destiny of the whole world.

According to Balaam's vision all the *goyim*, all the wicked
nations of the earth, the sons of Seth, Amalek, and Edom will
be hit. The event is situated at the time of the end, until he
perishes (Num 24:20, 24). The expression is repeated twice,
to hammer on the absolute eradication of evil. Obadiah's
prophecy echoes Balaam's words, and in a cosmic perspective
refers to Edom, as a symbol of all the nations who opposed God
and His people, to announce the ultimate victory of God and

---

36. See *Baalei Tossafot Ex.* 1:8.

the coming of the new age: "the kingdom shall be the Lord's" (Obad 21). The survival of the righteous is thus intricately connected to the destiny of the whole world. Salvation implies necessarily a cosmic scenario.

The messianic hope that Balaam "saw" was not about what could be built in the walls of this dust; it was not a hope forging the human dream and effort. It was the vision of "new heavens and earth" (Isa 65:17), a new order where only the righteous will be.

CHAPTER III

THE SIGN

Hear now, O house of David!
Is it a small thing to weary men,
But will you weary my God also?
Therefore the Lord Himself will give you a sign:
Behold, the virgin shall conceive and bear a Son
And shall call His name Immanuel
(Isa 7:13–14)

This oracle of Isa 7:14 is given in the historical context of the encounter between the prophet Isaiah and Ahaz, king of Judah (735–715 B.C.E.), right after Isaiah had received his call as a prophet (chap. 6), and against the background of a sinful Israel (1:4, 5:7) expecting unavoidable judgment and punishment (5:8–30). Judgment will come from the North: Rezin, the king of Aram (Syria), and Pekah, king of Samaria (the northern tribes of Israel), threatened to march against Judah with every intent of crushing the Jewish kingdom and replacing the son of David with the son of Tabeel (Isa 7:6). Thus, the Davidic dynasty, and hence the messianic line, is endangered. This is why the prophetic oracle points directly at the whole "house of David" (7:13). First, the prophet Isaiah tries to reassure Ahaz:

Do not fear or be fainthearted for these two stubs of
smoking firebrands. (Isa 7:4)

It shall not stand, nor shall it come to pass. (Isa 7:7)

Yet the king remains skeptical, as evidenced by the
prophet's remarks: "If you will not believe, surely you shall
not be established" (7:9). Therefore, the prophet offers the test
of a sign, which Ahaz turns down:

"Ask a sign for yourself from the Lord your God: ask
it either in the depth or in the height above." But Ahaz
said, "I will not ask, nor will I test the Lord!" (7:11–12)

Ahaz's response sounds orthodox, since he refers to the
Torah's principle enjoining not to tempt the Lord (Deut 6:16;
Ps 78:18). The truth of the matter is that Ahaz had already
planned to join the coalition of rebellion against Egypt and had
probably already sent off messengers to Assyria for help (see 2
Kgs 16). So, Ahaz does not need God's help and does not wish
to run the risk of faith and trust the God of heavens.

The voice of the prophet articulates, then, in this tragic void:
"Therefore [*lakhen*] the Lord Himself will give you a sign" (Isa
7:14). God's sign for the future is given as a direct response to
Ahaz's rejection of the future. It is as if Ahaz had refused to be
involved in the messianic construction of the messianic seed.
Ahaz said no to the future of the Davidic line. The prophecy
is given in response to Ahaz's negation: "Therefore . . . a virgin shall conceive and bear a son" (Isa 7:14). The exegesis of
this passage stumbles on a number of difficult questions. The
first issue concerns, obviously, the nature and the identity of this
woman who gives birth. Is this woman really a virgin, as it has

been understood by the Greek version of the Septuagint and supported in Christian tradition? Or, is she simply a young woman referring to a contemporary lady, the king's own wife, or even Isaiah's own wife, as most scholars think? Depending on the answer to this first question about the identity of the woman, one shall be able to answer the second question regarding the identity of the son who is born. Is he the son of a contemporary king, for instance Hezekiah[1]; or is he the son of the prophet Isaiah[2]; or is he the future Messiah Himself? Or, is this text having a dual application, referring both to a historical contemporary figure and to the future Messiah? In that case, is the historical figure to be understood as a type anticipating the ideal messianic figure (typological approach),[3] or reversely, is the messianic interpretation of this passage a mere re-application of the historical figure, and would, then, be free from the "actual meaning of the passages"[4] (re-reading approach)? In order to probe these questions, and as far as possible, trace the messianic intention of this text, we will interrogate the text as it is, that is with its words and syntax and in its specific literary context and expressions.

1. See A. Alt, "Jesaja 8,23–9,6. Befreiungsmacht und Krönungstag," in *Festschrift Alfred Bertholet gewidmet,* ed. W. Baumgartner (Tübingen: Mohr Siebeck, 1950), 29–49. Cf. Magnus Zetterholm, *The Messiah in Early Judaism and Christianity* (Minneapolis, MN: Fortress Press, 2007), 4.

2. See W. Grogan, "Isaiah," in *Expositor's Bible Commentary*, ed. Tremper Longman III and David E. Garland, rev. ed. (Grand Rapids, MI: Zondervan, 2008), 6:62–63.

3. See Richard M. Davidson, "The Messianic Hope in Isaiah 7:14 and the Volume of Immanuel (Isaiah 7–12)," in *"For You Have Strengthened Me" Biblical and Theological Studies in Honor of Gerhard Pfandl in Celebration of His Sixty-Fifth Birthday,* ed. Martin Pröbstle with assistance of Gerald A. Klingbeil and Martin G. Klingbeil (St. Peter am Hart, Austria: Seminar Schloss Bogenhoffen, 2007), esp. 92 (cf. 89, n. 15).

4. John Goldgingay, *Isaiah*, New International Biblical Commentary (Peabody, MA: Hendrickson, 2001), 67.

Poetic Analysis

The oracle is inserted within the literary context of God's address to Ahaz in an ABA[1] structure starting in 7:3 and ending in 7:17.[5]

A   God to Ahaz (2nd person masculine singular), vv. 3–12
- Reference to Shear-Jashub (present sign of hope from here)
- Threat and deliverance from the two kings

   B   God to the house of David (2nd person masculine plural), vv. 13–14
- Future birth of a child (sign from God): Immanuel

A[1]   God to Ahaz (2nd person masculine singular), vv. 15–25
- Referring to the child as a present sign from here (Shear-Jashub)
- Threat and deliverance from the two kings

The ABA[1] structure of God's addresses is determined according to the respective addressee and contents. Thus, the literary connection between A (vv. 3–12) and A[1] (vv. 15–25) is based on the facts that (1) both A and A[1] contain God's address to King Ahaz and therefore speak in the second person singular[6] (A—four times in vv. 45, 11; A[1]—four times in vv. 16–17, 25); (2) both elaborate on the threat from the SyroEphraimite forces and the deliverance from them; (3) both imply the actual presence of a son as a sign of hope.

---

5. In the following verses (18–25), the prophetic word turns into four independent oracles of doom relating to Assyria. Each is introduced by a fixed prophetic formula, "in that day" (18, 20–21, 23).

6. The use of the plural form in "if you will not believe, you shall not be established" in 7:9 may be explained as "a general maxim that applies to everyone" (John D. W. Watts, *Isaiah 1–33*, Word Biblical Commentary, vol. 24 [Waco, TX: Word, Inc., 1985], 93).

On the other hand, God's address in vv. 13–14 (B) is distinctive from A and A[1] in that it (1) concerns more broadly the house of David and speaks therefore in the second person plural (four times in vv. 13–14); (2) it does not refer to any external threat, but rather to the relationship between God and the house of David; (3) the child of this oracle is not yet born; he belongs to the future and is a sign of hope from God.

The Virgin

The problem of this text is, first of all, a linguistic one and concerns the meaning of the Hebrew word *'almah* ("virgin"). Does this word really mean virgin? This particular meaning has been challenged on the basis of the following argument: If Isaiah indeed meant "virgin," why did he choose the word *'almah* which is used only nine times in the Hebrew Bible and carries an ambiguous meaning (virgin or young woman)? Why did he not use instead the technical word *betulah*, which is used 51 times in the Hebrew Bible with the allegedly unambiguous meaning of "virgin"?

First of all, it should be noticed that it is not correct to say that the word *betulah* means unambiguously "virgin." The word also refers to a nonvirgin woman. This sense is attested in Ugaritic literature where the word *betulah* designates the goddess Anat who happens to have had sexual intercourse repeatedly.[7] In the Hebrew Bible, only three of the 51 occurrences of *betulah* mean unambiguously "virgin" (Lev 21:13; Deut 22:19; Ezek 44:22) and once it clearly does not, in Joel 1:8, where the *betulah* weeps about the husband of her youth. From the other passages, it is

---

7. See Adrianus van Selms, *Marriage and Family Life in Ugaritic Literature* (London: Luzac, 1954), 69, 109.

difficult to determine whether the biblical author meant actual virginity. The very fact that the word *betulah* is sometimes accompanied by the phrase no man had known her[8] may even suggest that the use of this word *betulah* was not explicit enough since it needed that specification.

On the other hand, it is remarkable that in none of the passages where the word *'almah* occurs it is applied to a married woman.[9] The biblical evidence then suggests that the word *'almah,* more than the word *betulah,* could be qualified to express the idea of virginity. Actually, it is only later, in the legal contexts of rabbinic literature, that the word *betulah* acquired the technical meaning of "virgin." It is, therefore, a mistake to read the biblical word *betulah* with the exclusive rabbinic meaning in mind.

As we already indicated, the biblical document shows that at that time the idea of virginity was expressed through the word *'almah* rather than through the word *betulah*. When Isaiah used the word *betulah,* it was to express a special concept. In the book of Isaiah, indeed, the singular word *betulah* appears four times. In all the four texts,[10] the word is used with the classical meaning as an archetype for people, once referring to Babylon, once to Sidon, and twice to Judah.[11] Isaiah used the word *'almah*

---

8. Gen 24:16; Judg 21:12; Lev 21:3.

9. Gen 24:16 (*betulah*), 43 (*'almah*); Exod 2:8; Ps 68:26 [25]; Prov 30:19; Song 1:3; 6:8.

10. Isa 23:12; 37:22; 47:1; 62:5. In Isa 23:4, the word is used a fifth time with the plural form and refers to particular women.

11. These numerous biblical instances where *betulah* is a personification of a nation or a city have been explained as "expansions or playful modifications of the frequent two-word expressions . . . *bath yehudhah*, 'daughter of Judah' . . . *bath 'ammi*, 'daughter of my people,' etc." (M. Tsevat, "*bethûlh*," in *Theological Dictionary of the Old Testament*, ed. G. Johannes Botterweck and Helmer Ringgren (Grand Rapids, MI: Eerdmans, 1974), 2:341).

in chap. 7, rather than *betulah,* in order to avoid the possible confusion with the other meaning of *betulah*, because he meant here a particular woman. If the word *betulah* had been used, considering its particular usage in the book, it might have been misunderstood as a corporate reference to Zion.

Actually, the use of the definite article with the word "virgin" may support the interpretation of the virginity of the woman in question, since the definite article is often used in a generic sense to refer to "classes or species" that "are unique."[12] In this instance, the use of the definite article suggests the special and unique category the "virgin" represents. Also, the fact that this future son was to be born from a particular virgin woman, fits quite well with the expressed intention to give this birth as a prophetic sign for the supernatural intervention of God. For, if the text did not intend a birth from a virgin woman, how could a natural birth from a regular woman such as Ahaz's wife or Isaiah's wife be then interpreted as a sign of the supernatural?

Yet beyond the strictly literary context of the biblical text, the mysterious language of this oracle, the perspective of hope, the proclamation of a marvelous birth involving a virgin, and even the use of the Hebrew word *'almah*, all this carries special connotations in regard to the cultural context of the ancient Middle East. Surprisingly, this strange resonance evokes the ancient Canaanite myth of a virgin woman who would give birth to a god. Six centuries before Isaiah, the Phoenician texts of Ras Shamra contain almost word for word the same phrase and even the same word *'alma*:

---

12. See Paul Joüon, *A Grammar of Biblical Hebrew*, vol. 2, trans. and rev. T. Muraoka (Rome: Editrice Pontifico Biblico, 2000), § 137i.

A virgin (*betulah*) will give birth
A damsel (*'almah*) will bear a son[13]

Although this birth belongs here to a context that is purely mythological within a cosmic religion referring to the birth of a cosmic god, the sun for instance, the annunciation formula in Isaiah belongs on the contrary to the real scene of history. The prophet intervenes on a particular and precise occasion; his action is political and not magical or mythological. The sign he offers is like the other signs, his two sons, a real sign pointing to a real event that belongs to real human history: the virgin and the son are not allegories or spiritual categories, but human beings who will exist in time, just as the two kings who threaten Israel. It is quite possible that Isaiah used this well-known motif in the ancient Middle East to convey his message. Besides confirming the meaning of "virgin" for the word *'almah*,[14] the parallels between the two texts reinforce the supernatural atmosphere that surrounds this birth and the identity of this child.

The Child

The supernatural character of this birth is also indicated in the very name of the child: Immanuel, "God with us." The specific context of this passage suggests indeed that the names that are here given prophetically are to be taken seriously, and even literally. For they really mean what they say. Thus,

---

13. C. H. Gordon, *Ugaritic Handbook: Revised Grammar, Paradigms, Texts in Transliteration, Comprehensive Glossar* (Rome: Pontificium Institutum Biblicum, 1947), text 77, Line 7.

14. See the discussion of R. K. Harrison, *Introduction to the Old Testament* (Grand Rapids, MI: Eerdmans, 1975), 482–483.

the meaning of the first son's name Shear-Jashub, "remnant shall return" (Isa 7:3), is a word of hope,[15] a promise assuring a physical return from battle or deportation Isa 6:12–13). Likewise, the meaning of the second son's name Maher-Shalal-Hash-Baz, "Speed the Spoil, Hasten the Booty," points to the defeat of Damascus and Samaria (Isa 8:4). Just as the names of these two sons are given as signs pointing to a real fulfillment in history, the name of Immanuel, "God with us," should therefore be understood as a real fulfillment in history and not just as a vague "spiritual" application. The birth of this child is supposed to bring God closer to us, in fact, "with us." The promise of God's presence with us serves as the actual evidence that God will respond and will be present in Ahaz's history.

The purpose of this future supernatural birth is to ensure, then, that the Davidic line will not be aborted in spite of Ahaz's rejection, and above all, in spite of the military threats. Now, the crucial question about this child concerns his identity: Is he the prophet's son? Is he the son of King Ahaz? Or is he the future Son of David, Messiah of Israel?

1. This son cannot be the prophet's son since the prophet's wife already had a son Shear-Jashub (Isa 7:3) and could, therefore, not qualify as a virgin. Also, the name of the child (Immanuel) is given by his mother (Isa 7:14) and not by the prophet, a peculiarity that indicates that he cannot be the prophet's son; for it was the prophet himself who normally

---

15. The context of God's reassuring words, "be quiet; do not fear" (Isa 7:3 [ET 4]) and the prediction that the king's enemies will be broken (Isa 7:8–9) suggests that only the positive reading of the name Shear-Yashub should be retained (against Watts, 91; and John Goldingay, *Isaiah*, New International Biblical Commentary [Peabody, MA: Hendrickson, 2001], 64).

gave the name to his son (Isa 8:3). This reference to the
mother is all the more striking as the prophet is speaking
to a man, the king, who had just responded negatively to
God's sign. This response is also given in direct response
to the king's refusal, hence the use of the word "therefore"
(*lachen*) introducing God's response. It sounds like an
irony: since the king of Israel refuses to be involved in
Gods plan, the child will be conceived without "his" help,
without any males help: "the virgin shall conceive and bear
a son." Ahaz is, therefore, naturally excluded as the father
of that son. This prophecy, which speaks about a future
birth, also eliminates the option of his son Hezekiah "who
was apparently born some years before"[16] and whose birth
was not from a virgin mother anyway.

2. The name of the son receives a prophetic meaning,
   Immanuel ("God with us"), like the names of the two other
   prophet's sons; but unlike the names of the prophet's sons,
   Immanuel's name is *theophorous*;[17] it bears the name of
   God, thus referring to the divine realm, while the names
   of the prophet's sons limit this vision to the scope of the
   history of Israel, alluding to the return of the people from
   the Babylonian exile: Shear-Jashub means "a remnant"
   "will return," Maher-Shalal-Hash-Baz means "speed the
   spoil, hasten the booty."

3. Unlike the other sons whose fathers are clearly identified
   as the prophet Isaiah (Isa 7:3; 8:3), or as Ahaz (2 Kgs
   16:20; 2 Chr 28:27), Immanuel's father is never identified.

---

16. Goldingay, *Isaiah*, 67.
17. Although the name of Hezekiah is *theophorous* (meaning "Yahweh is my
strength"), it is not given as a prophetic name.

4. The literary structure of the divine address (see above) brings out the Immanuel passage (B: Isa 7:14) in sharp contrast to the other two passages (A: Isa 7:3–12 and A^1: Isa 7:15–25). In these two passages (A and A^1), the reference to the child is associated with the local present history of Israel (the threat from the two kings), and Ahaz is there directly addressed in the second person masculine singular, whereas in the Immanuel passage (B), the reference to the child transcends the local history of Ahaz and opens to a wider horizon: it addresses the house of David. That is to say, that in B the sign is not intended towards Ahaz, who had already turned down God's offer for a sign, but instead to the house of David. It is a sign, which concerns all the kings of the house of David, a sign that the throne of David will not be empty. Therefore, this sign belongs to the future.[18] Immanuel is not given as a sign of the present to speak about the future, as a type of the future Messiah. He is the Messiah Himself. The birth of the Messiah, son of David, the ultimate descendant of David, is the sign from the future, the guarantee from there that the Davidic line will not be disrupted; it is a sign from the future of the particular presence of the Lord among his people now. Interestingly, this is the very lesson that was supposed to be understood by Israel of that time who was threatened by the Assyrian armies. The phrase *Immanuel* "God with us," which spoke of the future, was re-applied to illuminate the present situation (Isa 8:8, 10). In that

---

18. For biblical examples of a sign located in the future, see, for instance, Exod 3:12; 1 Sam 2:34; Jer 44:29–30. See also, F. J. Helfmeyer, "'*oth*," in *Theological Dictionary of the Old Testament*, ed. G. Johannes Botterweck and Helmer Ringgren (Grand Rapids, MI: Eerdmans, 1974), 1:183–184.

sense the messianic interpretation belongs to the historical context of our passage. It is not correct, then to say that "it ignores the rightful demands of contextual and historical exegesis, which call for a meaning, related to the end of the Syro-Ephraimite war."[19]

Isaiah 7:14 in the Hebrew Bible

Isaiah 9:5–6

The strong echoes between the Immanuel passage of Isa 7:13–14 and Isa 9:5–6, some of them being exclusive to those two passages, suggest that the child Immanuel of Isa 7:14 is the same person as the child referred to in Isa 9:6–7 (Heb. 9:5–6):

> For unto **us** a **Child is born**, unto **us** a **Son is given**; and the government will be upon His shoulder. And His **name will be called** Wonderful, Counselor, Mighty **God**, Everlasting Father, Prince of Peace. Of the increase of His government and peace there will be no end, upon the throne of **David** and over His kingdom, to order it and establish it with judgment and justice from that time forward, even forever. The zeal of the Lord of hosts will perform this.

These two passages of Isaiah share a significant number of common motifs and wording (marked in bold in the above quotation). Both are prophetic declarations of the birth of a son (*ben*). In Isa 7:14, as in Isa 9:5–6, this birth is described as a gift from God to "us." In both cases, the verb "give" *(ntn)* is used

---

19. Watts, *Isaiah*, 104.

with God as the subject related to the personal pronoun "us" (*nu*). In Isa 9:6 (Heb. 9:5), the idea of birth is also rendered by a passive form, Pual and Niphal, verbal forms, which normally imply God as the subject.[20] In both passages, the son is called (*qr'*) with a prophetic name that refers to God Himself.

Furthermore, the two passages are complementary. In Isa 7:14 the name of the child refers to God's immanence and proximity, *Immanuel* ("God with us"); in Isa 9:6 the name of the child refers to God's power and transcendence, "Wonderful, Counselor, Mighty God, Everlasting Father, Prince of Peace" (Isa 9:6). Isa 7:14 refers just to the child, only as a sign of hope implicitly indicating to Ahaz and the people of that time that there will be an heir on the throne of David; our passage extends in space and in time, beyond the person of the child, to the level of the kingdom and of eternity and explicitly ensures that from this Son of David, "there will be no end upon the throne of David" (Isa 9:7).

Isaiah 11:12

Although this text does not contain clear linguistic echoes or parallels with Isa 7:14, the presence of the common theme of the supernatural Davidic birth suggests, at least, some spiritual connection between the two passages and should therefore be considered:

There shall come forth a Rod from the stem of Jesse,

and a Branch shall grow out of his roots,

---

20. See Jacques B. Doukhan, *Daniel, The Vision of the End*, 2nd ed., rev. (Berrien Springs, MI: Andrews University Press, 1989), 36.

The Spirit of the Lord shall rest upon Him,

The Spirit of wisdom and understanding,

The Spirit of counsel and might,

The Spirit of knowledge and of the fear of the Lord.

Among the thematic echoes between the two passages, one may think of the birth of the Davidic Messiah, which is here compared to the growth of a "rod," a "stem," a "branch" out of a felled tree[21] thus reminding of the Davidic birth from the virgin in Isa 7:14. In both cases the birth is miraculous and unexpected. The motif of the "sign" (*'oth*) that qualifies the messianic appearance in Isa 7:14, reappears in Isa 11:10, 12; only this time, instead of the technical word *'oth*, we have a synonym *nes,* here translated by "banner" but carrying the connotation of "sign" (see Ps 60:6 [Heb. 4]).

Also, the dual nature of the Messiah is again emphasized in Isa 11:1–2. Like in the two passages above, Isa 11:1–2 associates the theme of the Davidic origin and of the divine status of the Messiah. If his birth out of the stem of David ("stem of Jesse") indicates his human/royal descent, his spiritual attributes stress seven times his belonging to the divine realm, with an *inclusio* on "the Lord."

The Spirit of the Lord, of wisdom, of understanding, of counsel, might, of knowledge and of the fear of the Lord.

---

21. Cf. Goldingay, *Isaiah*, 83.

The messianic identity of this Son of David is further confirmed in the next few verses,which contain one of the greatest classics of the biblical texts of hope. The coming of this Son of David will indeed take us to the messianic era. A time of absolute peace between the creatures, which will not feel threatened any more:

> The wolf also shall dwell with the lamb,
>
> The leopard shall lie down with the young goat,
>
> The calf and the young lion and the fatling together,
>
> And a little child shall lead them.
>
> The cow and the bear shall graze,
>
> Their young ones shall lie down together;
>
> And the lion shall eat straw like an ox. (Isa 11:6–7)

A time of absolute life where there will be no harm any more:

> They shall not hurt nor destroy in all My holy mountain. (Isa 11:9).

Then the text gives the reason for this idyllic time, namely the effective presence of the Lord and the Son of David:

> For the earth shall be full of the knowledge of the Lord as the waters cover the sea
>
> And in that day there shall be a Root of Jesse. (Isa 11:9–10)

Micah 5:2–4

Outside the book of Isaiah, the same themes of supernatural birth and of hope reappear in Mic 5:2–4 as the prophet describes the coming of the future Davidic Messiah. In addition, the language of Micah is reminiscent of the language of Isaiah, sharing a significant number of common words (as evident in bold in the translation below and in the following transliteration):

Therefore the Lord Himself will give you a sign: Behold the virgin shall conceive and bear a son, and shall call **His name Immanuel**. (Isaiah 7:14)

Therefore He shall give them up, until the time she who is in labor has **given birth**; . . . And He shall stand and feed His flock in the strength of the Lord, in the majesty of the **name of the Lord His God;** and they shall abide, for now He shall be great to the ends of the earth; and this One shall be peace. (Mic 5:2–4)

lakhen yitten lakemn...	*lakhen yitnem...*
weyoledet	*yoledah*
shemo Immanuel	*shem Adonay Elohaw*
(Isa 7:14)	(Mic 5:2–3)

Undoubtedly, the text of Mic 5:2–3 alludes to Isa 7:14. Here also, the future Redeemer belongs to the Davidic branch (He comes from Bethlehem; 5:2); and here, also, His birth is supernatural since it originates as a gift of God and in the eternity of God, "whose goings forth have been from of old, from everlasting" (5:2); and lastly, here also the birth is associated with redemption and placed in the perspective of universal peace (5:4).

Summary

The analysis of Isa 7:14 with the enrichment of its parallel texts suggests the following lessons regarding the extraordinary birth of the Messiah:

1. The birth of the Messiah will be supernatural since His conception will not involve the participation of a male; the "virgin" will be pregnant. This birth is given to Ahaz as God's sign from the future, not only to respond to Ahaz's refusal, but also to reassure the house of David. The promise of the future birth of the messianic descendant of David is a sign of hope for the present Israelite community, a sign that their enemies will be vanquished and a sign that the throne of David will be occupied. The messianic hope meets the concern of the people of that time. The messianic interpretation fits therefore the historical context of this biblical passage.

2. The birth of the Messiah will bring the presence of God among humans as indicated by (a) His prophetic name, *Immanuel*, "God with us"; (b) His prophetic titles, "mighty God," "everlasting Father" (Isaiah 9:6); (c) His spiritual attributes, "the Spirit of the Lord upon Him" (Isa 11:2); (d) His origin "from everlasting" (Mic 5:3) and (e) His accomplishment, "the wolf shall dwell with the lamb" (Isa 11: 6).

3. The birth of the Messiah will be supernatural (from a virgin) as well as natural (it will be a birth from the stem of Jesse/David), immanent "with us" as well as transcendent *El*, in time (a sign for the present given from the future) as well as in eternity ("everlasting Father" and "from everlasting"). The Messiah will then mysteriously combine the incompatible human and divine orders within Himself.

Isaiah 7:14 in Jewish Tradition

The Septuagint

The Septuagint, the Greek translation of Isa 7:14 confirms that the birth implied here should be supernatural since the Greek word to qualify the mother is *parthenos*, a technical word for "virgin," which the Septuagint uses generally to translate the Hebrew word *bethulah* (Exod 22:16; Job 31:1; Isa 23:4, etc.) but also *na'arah* (Gen 24:43; Isa 7:14) when these words designate a virgin.

Qumran

One of the thanksgiving hymns (I QH III) combines both the Hebrew texts of Isa 7:14 and Isa 9:5 (ET 6) to evoke the birth of the Messiah:[22]

> She shall bring forth a man-child, and amid the pains of Hell there shall spring from her childbearing crucible a Marvelous Mighty Counselor.[23]

Talmud

The messianic weight of Isa 7:14 was such that some rabbis of the early Talmudic period were persuaded that the Messiah had already come in the time of Hezekiah. Thus, Hillel in the first century C.E. said:

> There shall be no Messiah for Israel, because they have already enjoyed him in the days of Hezekiah.[24]

---

22. On this text, see André Dupont-Sommer, *The Essene Writings from Qumran*, trans. G. Vermes (Gloucester, MA: Peter Smith, 1973), 208, n.1.

23. 23Presented by Geza Vermes in *The Dead Sea Scrolls in English*, 3rd ed. (London: Penguin Books, 1987), 171.

24. *B. Sanhedrin* 98b and 99a, as quoted from H. Freedman, ed. and trans., *Sanhedrin: Translated into English with Notes, Glossary and Indices* (London: Soncino Press, 1935), 669.

It is interesting that this text is not explicitly referred to as a messianic passage, maybe because of the intense Jewish-Christian polemic about it. Yet the very ingredient that made this verse controversial and suspect from a Jewish point of view, namely the supernatural birth, has strangely been preserved in the rabbinic memory. Indeed, the rabbis of the Talmud went so far as to suggest that the Messiah was more than human and Davidic. Bearing the name of God, the Messiah was identified with God Himself:

> The Messiah will have the name of the Holy Blessed One[25] . . . for it is said in Jeremiah 23:6: "And this is the name by which he will be called: 'The Lord is our righteousness.'" (*Baba bathra* 75b)

Midrash

The ancient rabbis were bold enough to describe the birth of the Messiah as a mysterious conception from above.

> The Redeemer that I shall bring forth one day will be without father, as it has been said: "Behold a man whose name is seed[26] and he shall germinate by his own means"; even as Isaiah has said: "He rose up before him even as a seed, as a shoot that comes forth from dry land" . . . And it is of him that the

---

25. This is the common designation of God in Rabbinic literature.

26. The seed or shoot is one of the most dominant images in the Rabbinic literature for evoking the person of the Messiah (cf. *y. Berakoth* 5a; some texts of *Numbers Rabbah* 18 on Numbers 15:35; *Genesis Rabbah* 23:5 on Genesis 4:25 [*Genesis*, trans. H. Freedman, Midrash Rabbah (London: Soncino Press, 1939), 196]; in the latter Midrash, King Messiah is conceived as "that seed which would arise from another source").

Scripture says: "Behold, this day have I begotten thee." (*Bereshit Rabbati* on Genesis 37:22).

The Midrash attests to the same reasoning:

To the question, "What is the name of the Messiah King?" Rabbi Abba ben Kahana answers: "Yahweh is his name as written in Jeremiah 23:6, 'this is the name by which he will be called: The Lord [*YHWH*] is our righteousness.'" (*Eikha Rabbati* 1 on Lamentations 1:16)

On Zephaniah 3:9, "I will restore to the peoples a pure language that they may all call on the name of *YHWH*, to serve Him with one accord": the "name of *YHWH*" is nothing but the King Messiah. (*Bereshit Rabbati* 41:44)

"And the Spirit of God was hovering" (Genesis 1:2), it is the Spirit of the King Messiah. (*Berishit Rabbah* 2:5)

These statements are indeed surprising and perhaps disturbing in view of the Jewish-Christian polemic. Today such ideas would be deemed suspect, betraying a biased Christian apologetic. But they should be received as they are, namely, as plain witnesses to the historical fact that the messianic interpretation of Isa 7:14, and more specifically the belief of a supernatural birth excluding the male involvement was not absent in Jewish tradition.

Parallel Texts of Isaiah 7:14 Recognized as Messianic in Jewish Tradition

Isaiah 9:5-6

The prophet said to the house of David: "a master was born to us, a son has been given to us; He will take the Torah upon Him to keep it; His name has been pronounced since the beginning: Wonderful Counselor, Mighty God, Existing Eternally, Messiah in which days the peace will abound." (*Targum* on Isaiah 9:5)

Chapter of *shalom* ("peace"), chapter 10. Rabbi Jose the Galilean said: "the name of the Messiah will be called *Shalom* ('Peace'), for it is written in Isaiah 9:5 [9:6], 'his name will be called Everlasting Father, Prince of Peace'" . . . Rabbi Jose the Galilean said also: "When the Messiah will come, peace will be great and there will be redemption for Israel." (*Dereq Erets Zutha, Pereq 10*)

I have yet to raise the King Messiah on whom it is written in Isaiah 9:6 "unto us a Child is born." (*Debarim Rabbah* 1: 17)

Isaiah 11:1-2

The King will come out of Jesse, and the Messiah from the sons of his son will be exalted. (*Targum* of Isaiah 11:1)

> It is written of the Messiah in Isaiah 11:2, the Spirit of the Lord will rest on Him, Spirit of Wisdom and Intelligence, Spirit of Counsel and Strength. (*Talmud, Sanhedrin* 93a)

> Rabi Eliezer said "God grounded the earth with three qualities, Wisdom, Understanding and Knowledge; these three qualities have been given to the King Messiah, as it is said in Is 11:2 'the Spirit of the Lord shall rest upon Him, Spirit of Wisdom, etc.'" (*Bereshit Rabbati* Genesis 1:2)

According to Jewish tradition, in tune with the biblical data, the Messiah could be identified with God Himself. Savior, eternal, supreme King, the Lord, *Adonai* Himself endowed with the Spirit of God; but at the same time, he could also be identified with the son of David, the son of Jesse. What will become inconceivable and irreconcilable later in Judaism was yet perfectly acceptable at the early stages of rabbinic thinking.

For renowned scholar Raphael Patai, the divine dimension of the Messiah is what characterizes Jewish traditions about the Messiah more than anything; thus he notes in his introduction to his *Messiah Texts* that "in comparison with other myths, this feature is most intensively and emphatically present in the Messiah myth." According to Patai, it is this combination of the divine and the human that "lends the myth much of its tension, power, and enduring, fateful influence."[27] After a thorough examination of ancient Jewish literature, this is also the surprising conclusion of Jewish scholar David Flusser, of the Hebrew University of Jerusalem: "In the Midrashic

---

27. Raphael Patai, *The Messiah Texts* (Detroit, MI: Wayne State University Press, 1988), L.

literature, the ways of the Messiah acquire a dimension which is beyond everyday life and passes human understanding."[28]

Isaiah 7:14 in the New Testament

The book of Isaiah is, after the book of the Psalms, the book that is the most quoted or alluded to in the New Testament. Significantly, the first quotation of the Old Testament in the New Testament is Isa 7:14; it is found in the context of the birth proclamation of Jesus in:

Matt 1:20–23:

> Behold, an angel of the Lord appeared to him in a dream, saying, "Joseph, son of David, do not be afraid to take to you Mary your wife, for that which is conceived in her is of the Holy Spirit. And she will bring forth a Son, and you shall call His name Jesus, for He will save His people from their sins." Now all this was done that it might be fulfilled which was spoken by the Lord through the prophet, saying: "Behold, a virgin shall be with child, and bear a Son, and they shall call His name Immanuel" which is translated, "God with us."

Besides the literal quotation of Isa 7:14, it is interesting to notice that the birth proclamation of Jesus in our Matthew text contains a number of significant parallels with the birth proclamation of Immanuel in Isa 7:1014. In both texts, indeed, the Lord speaks to the husband of the future mother and in both texts the house of David is addressed. In both texts the husband is reassured and urged not to fear (Isa 7:4,

---

28. David Flusser, "The Concept of the Messiah," in *Jewish Sources in Early Christianity* (New York: Adam Books, 1987), 56.

cf. Matt 1:20). The only difference is that unlike Ahaz, who refuses the miracle and does not give the name of Immanuel, Joseph, who accepts it, will give the name of Jesus. There was no problem for Matthew in applying the name Immanuel to Jesus since it was not considered a personal name but was rather received as a phrase describing the task this Messiah would—perform an understanding which was already implied in the other occurrences of Immanuel in Isaiah (see Isa 8:8, 10).

The same message of the name "God with us" may also be intended in Matt 28:20, where the last words of Jesus conclude the Gospel: "I am with you always, even to the end of the age."

The Messianic Birth

Jewish tradition attests to the idea of a supernatural birth for the Messiah precisely on the basis of Eve's birth report of Seth:

> She called him Seth, for she said, "God has given [*shet*] me another posterity," which means, as R. Tanhuma observed in the name of R. Samuel: "Eve saw the seed which comes from another place, and what is it? It is the King Messiah." (*Ber Rabbah* 23:7)

That the messianic seed originates "from another place," which is outside of the human sphere, is in itself an indication, a "sign," of the supernatural nature of the messianic birth. It is interesting to note that in the Bible messianic salvation has consistently been connected to the supernatural nature of human birth. This principle is already present in the history of Israel in general where the salvation of the people is associated with God's special and supernatural intervention on human births. When Pharaoh's oppression was designed to keep Israel from growing, and the midwives were instructed to kill all the newborn sons, "God dealt well with the midwives, and the people multiplied and grew very mighty" (Exod 1:20). Significantly, the birth of Moses, the future deliverer of Israel took place in that very context, and the baby was miraculously rescued from the water (Exod 2:1–10). Likewise, the birth of the judge Samson, who will save Israel from the Philistines, is surrounded with supernatural activities. The woman who was supposed to conceive and give birth to him "was barren and had no children. And the Angel of the Lord appeared to the woman and said to her: 'Indeed now, you are barren and have borne no children, but you shall conceive and bear a son'" (Judg 13:23). It is the same scenario concerning the birth of Samuel whose wife "Hannah could not have children; she prayed and God responded: Hannah conceived and bore a son, and called his name Samuel, saying, 'because I have asked for him from the Lord.'"

But the supernatural and divine intervention in human birth is particularly at work in messianic salvation. The Messiah should come from the seed of the woman (Gen 3:15), a process that is recognized by Eve herself, who refers to God when she gives birth for the first time (Gen 4:1), and reaffirms this hope when she gives birth to Seth, the only son left to channel the messianic seed, which, she says, has been "put" (*shat*) by God Himself (Gen 4:25). The messianic line continues, through the seed of Jacob (Num 24:7, 17), and then through the seed of David (2 Sam 7:12–13; Mic 5:12; Isa 7:13–14). The physical evidence, the visible "sign" of God's presence with us is that this seed is not given as the result of a natural process. The births, which mark and construct the messianic line, generally imply supernatural intervention on God's part. This is the case for old Sarah (Gen 17:19), the infertile Rebecca (Gen 25:21), the unloved Leah (Gen 30:31), the Moabite Ruth (Ruth 4:11–13), and even Bathsheba whose previous son had died (2 Sam 12:24-25); all those women who were not supposed to give birth received the good news of their future unexpected pregnancy as a miracle and a sign of God's mercy and love. The messianic seed is, therefore, not conceived naturally. It is a seed that is initiated and controlled by God Himself. This is why birth plays such an important role in the Bible. It is not just because of its sociological function, or because of its fundamental place in family life, but more importantly it is because it involves the particular presence of God Himself, in connection to the event of salvation. It is already significant that the first time that God blesses it is in association with birth, first concerning the birth of the animals:

> So God created great sea creatures and every living thing that moves, with which the waters abounded . . . and every winged bird . . . And God **blessed** them, saying, **be fruitful**, and **fill** the waters in the seas, and let birds **multiply** on the earth. (Gen 1:21–22)

Then the same blessing is repeated in connection to human births:

> So God created man . . . male and female he created them. Then God **blessed** them, and God said to them, **be fruitful** and multiply, **fill** the earth. (Gen 1:27–28)

102

It is noteworthy that the first human births, which follow immediately the prophetic text of Gen 3:15, are recorded as involving directly God Himself; this time God does not just bless the birth from outside, He is present within the very process of birth:

> Now Adam knew Eve his wife, and she conceived and bore Cain, and said, "I have gotten a man from the Lord." (Gen 4:1)

> And Adam knew his wife again, and she bore a son and named him Seth, "For God has appointed another seed for me instead of Abel, whom Cain killed." (Gen 4:25)

The divine association with birth will continue later throughout the patriarchal period and the history of Israel. But this reference to God does not mean that the divine blessing is merely related to nature and creation. The essential reason for this supernatural evocation has to do with the future of history and is pregnant with salvation.[29] This is particularly obvious in the first blessing to Abram:

> I will make you a great nation, I will bless you
>
> and make your name great: and you shall be a blessing . . .
>
> And in you all the families of the earth shall be blessed. (Gen 12:23)

---

29. See Josef Scharbert, "*brk*," in *Theological Dictionary of the Old Testament,* ed. G. Johannes Botterweck and Helmer Ringgren (Grand Rapids, MI: Eerdmans, 1974), 2:306–307.

103

God does not just bless Abraham through the process of births; "I will make you a great nation" but all the nations of the earth will be blessed through that blessing. Universal salvation is thus constructed through these divinely blessed births.

The idea of God's direct involvement in the birth of a human being is, therefore, not so strange to biblical thinking. Following the births of the first humans, the births of patriarchs, Isaac (Gen 21), Jacob (Gen 25) and the son's of Jacob (Gen 29) are traced to God's will and supernatural interventions. It is through births that God enters, shapes, and guides history. It is significant that the word "genealogies," *toledot*, which means "giving birth," is used to designate God's act of creation (Gen 2:4), as well as human births that unfold in the meanders of history. Thus, the use of the term *toledot*, "generations," "begettings," in combination with genealogies in the sense of tribal history, could be interpreted "as a structural signal that the sacral history leading up to the people of Israel is being dealt with."[30] The births of the sons of the prophets were to signify God's action in history (Hos 1:4, 6, 9). Yet human birth was always received as God's gift and the manifestation of His blessing (Gen 1:28; 5:13). It remains, however, that the Hebrew Scriptures clearly describe procreation and birth as a natural human activity. On the other hand, it is noteworthy that when it comes to the birth of the king, the language is quite different and often suggests a divine origin. In a few passages God is given as the direct subject of the verb *yld* "to give birth" (Deut 32:18; Pss 2:7; 110:3). In Ps 2:7, God says to the Davidic king: "Today I have begotten you."

---

30. J. Schreiner, "*yalad*," in *Theological Dictionary of the Old Testament,* ed. G. Johannes Botterweck and Helmer Ringgren (Grand Rapids, MI: Eerdmans, 1974), 6:79.

Generally scholars have interpreted this irregularity against a mythological background.[31] But could it be that this exceptional case was due instead to the simple fact that the royal births anticipated and figuratively pointed to the supernatural birth of the Davidic Messiah?

Thus, all the salvation of the world, all the universal wisdom, all the infinite, and all the eternity should rest upon one particular man, (Isa 9:6) who will be begotten by a real woman and will live at a particular time in a particular place. That a particular man, who will exist historically, may carry in Himself "the Spirit of the Lord, the Spirit of Wisdom and Understanding, the Spirit of Counsel and Might, the Spirit of Knowledge" (Isa 11:2), that is all the spiritual, the universal truth, this is a scandal which hurts the most profound and rational inclinations of our Greek mind. That all the divinity would dwell physically in a particular individual is to bring together the two entities that Greek dualism had infinitely separated, the spiritual and the material. The wonder of "God with us," the presence of the Lord in history and in existence, the *Shekinah* that dwells among the people, this is indeed the nerve of Hebrew thinking. "God with us" does not mean, however, that a man will become divine through an upward movement. The finite or the mortal cannot elevate itself to the infinite or to the eternal status. But it means, instead, that the God of eternity will come down and shrink Himself in human existence, even through the reduction of birth, and the pains of suffering and the risk of annihilation through death so that we humans may have access to life and eternity.

---

31. P. Humbert, "Yahvé dieu géniteur?" *Asiatische Studien* 18, no.19 (1965): 250.

CHAPTER IV

THE SERVANT

Behold, My Servant shall deal prudently,
He shall be exalted and extolled and be very high . . .
Surely He has borne our griefs and carried our sorrows
Yet we esteemed Him stricken,
Smitten by God, and afflicted.
But He was wounded for our transgressions,
He was bruised for our iniquities;
The chastisement for our peace was upon Him,
And by His stripes we are healed.
All we like sheep have gone astray;
We have turned every one, to his own way;
And the Lord has laid on Him the iniquity of us all . . .
Therefore I will divide Him a portion with the great, and
He shall divide the spoil with the strong.
Because He poured out His soul unto death, and
He was numbered with the transgressors, and
He bore the sin of many, and made
Intercession for the transgressors.
(Isa 52:13–53:12)

The context of Isaiah's prophecy about the death of the "Suffering Servant" reminds one of the context of Isaiah's prophecy about the birth of the Messiah, Son of David. Both prophetic words are given against the same background of an encounter between the prophet Isaiah and a Judean king.

Yet they stand in striking and almost symmetric contrast to each other; in Isa 7, Isaiah met with King Ahaz; in Isa 39, Isaiah meets with King Hezekiah. Ahaz was a bad king who "did not do what was right in the sight of the Lord" as his father David had done (2 Chr 28:1). Hezekiah was a good king who "did what was right in the sight of the Lord, according to all that his father David had done" (2 Chr 29:2). While Ahaz does not pray to God for help, because of his alliance with the Assyrian world power and refuses the sign offered by God (Isa 7:11–12), Hezekiah prays to God for help against the same Assyrian world power (Isa 37:15–20) and even asks for a sign (Isa 38:22; 2 Kgs 20:8–11). While the message of Isa 7:14 sounds in the first section of Isaiah (1–39) as a word of judgment against the unfaithful King Ahaz and his sinful people, the message of the second section of Isaiah (40–66) sounds as a word of comfort responding to the faithful King Hezekiah in sorrow and his suffering people. The contrast between the two contexts is even reflected in the two prophecies. In Isa 7:14 the prophet predicts the birth of an individual whom he sees as a glorious-royal Figure originating both from the Davidic line and from God. In Isa 52:14–53:12, the prophet predicts the death of a suffering and humiliated Servant.[1]

---

1. This almost symmetrical contrast between the two sections of the book of Isaiah has been noticed by Rabbi Joseph Carlebach who spoke of two complementary perspectives (see Joseph Carlebach, *Die grossen Propheten: Jesaia, Jirmija und Jecheskel* [Frankfurt am Main: Hermon Verlag, 1932]); it also struck biblical scholar Wilhelm Vischer, who compared the book to an "ellipse" whose two foci were the word of "judgment" and the word of "comfort" (see Wilhelm Vischer, *Valeur de l'Ancien Testament* [Paris: Delachaux & Niestlé, 1958], 130).

One of the most perplexing questions of this passage concerns the identity of this Servant. This is not clear from the text itself. Sometimes the Servant clearly represents Israel, for the text explicitly designates Israel as a Servant (Isa 41:8–10; cf. 44:1–3, 21; 45:4; 48:21; 49:3). Sometimes the Servant is an individual clearly distinct from Israel (Isa 42:1–4; 49:1–7). Sometimes the text is ambiguous and does not explicitly designate the Servant. This is the case for the last Servant Song (Isa 52:13–53:13), where the situation is not as clear as in the other passages for the simple reason that the people of Israel are never explicitly named. The discussion of identification of this enigmatic figure has, therefore, continued from the first century, as attested in the Ethiopian's questions (Acts 8:34) until today's commentaries who still differ on that on that issue.[2] The most important point of contention that divides, then, the interpreters is whether the Servant is an individual or a corporate entity. And even within these two categories there is a great diversity of opinions. Traditional Christian interpreters tend to see a single individual of the future, Jesus himself. Traditional Jewish interpreters have generally seen the Servant as a symbol of Israel. Some like to see a historical figure of the past, Isaiah himself, Jeremiah, or a leader, Zerubbabel, Cyrus, Darius, whose suffering is interpreted as a symbol foreshadowing the person and the ministry of Jesus, or pointing to the suffering of the Jewish people. Others discern a specific group within the community of Israel, the spiritual

---

2. On the history of that discussion about the identity of the Suffering Servant, see C. R. North, *The Suffering Servant in Deutero-Isaiah* (London: Oxford University Press, 1948), esp. 192–219.

faithful remnant, whether in the Diaspora or in Judah. The reading of the biblical text as well as the reading of all these interpretations oblige our questions about the identity of the Suffering Servant: Who is the Suffering Servant of Isa 53? And what is his function? What does he signify? Is he representing Israel or is he someone distinct from Israel? Is he a historical figure of the past, contemporary to the biblical author or a prophetic figure of the future? All these questions should conduct our exegesis, our search and interrogations of the Hebrew text, our analysis of its poetic expression, and our close examination of its words and its stylistic expressions.

Poetic Analysis

This messianic prophecy is located at the end of a whole section in the book of Isaiah (40–53) often called the "Servant Songs," because the dominant figure is the "Servant of the Lord"; the term "servant" (*'ebed*) occurs there twenty times. Four songs have generally been recognized according to the following divisions:

1. 42:1–9

2. 49:1–13

3. 50:4–11

4. 52:13–53:12

The fourth song, which is the longest of all the Servant Songs, marks their literary and thematic climax.[3] The text is

---

3. See J. Alec Motyer, *The Prophecy of Isaiah: An Introduction and Commentary* (Downers Grove, IL: InterVarsity Press, 1993), 423; cf. Brevard S. Childs, *Isaiah*, Old Testament Library (Louisville, KY: Westminster John Knox Press, 2001), 410.

divided into five strophes of three verses each and follows a chiastic (or arch) structure as becomes obvious below:

A   Exaltation of the Servant (52:13–15)
    B   Humiliation of the Servant (53:1–3)
        C   Atonement by the Servant (53:4–6)
    B$_1$ Humiliation of the Servant (53:7–9)
A$_1$ Exaltation of the Servant (53:10–12)[4]

The literary construction suggests at least two lessons from the outset: (1) the fourth song is given as the most important moment, the climax of the prophetic discourse; (2) the atonement by the Servant, the idea that "He was wounded for our iniquities," placed as the apex of the chiasmus should therefore be identified as the central idea of the song, "its capsule synopsis," around which and on which basis the song would have been composed.[5]

The Suffering Servant and Israel

Considering the ambiguity of the qualification as "servant" which may apply to Israel as well as to an individual distinct from Israel and the absence of an explicit identification in the song, it is important as a preliminary to clarify the nature of the relationship between Israel and the Suffering Servant. Three data should play a role in that enquiry. First,

---

4. See Christopher R. North, *Isaiah 40–45: Introduction and Commentary* (London: SCM Press, 1952), 130; cf. F. Derek Kidner, "Isaiah," in *The Eerdmans Bible Commentary*, ed. D. Guthrie and J. A. Motyer, 3rd ed. (Grand Rapids, MI: Eerdmans, 1987), 618.

5. See R. L. Alden, "Is the High Point of a Psalm's Chiasmus the Point of the Psalm?" A paper read at the Society of Biblical Literature Annual Meeting, Chicago, IL, November 1988.

the directions indicated by the context and more precisely by the text that just precedes our passage and prepares for it. Second, the identity of those who speak. Third, the identity of those who hear.

1. The Directions of the Context

Just a few verses before, the biblical text was clearly and unambiguously referring to an individual distinct from Israel, someone who was called to save Israel:

> And the Lord says, who formed Me from the womb to be His Servant, to bring Jacob back to Him, so that Israel is gathered to Him (for I shall be glorious in the eyes of the Lord. And My God shall be my strength). Indeed He says, "it is too small a thing that you should be My Servant, to raise up the tribes of Jacob and to restore the preserved ones of Israel; I will also give you as a light to the Gentiles, that you should be my salvation to the ends of the earth." Thus says the Lord, the Redeemer of Israel, their Holy One, to Him whom man despises, to Him whom the nation abhors, to the Servant of rulers: "Kings shall see and arise, Princes also shall worship, because of the Lord who is faithful, the Holy One of Israel; and He has chosen you." (Isa 49:5–7)

Our passage makes a clear distinction between the people of Israel and the Servant. And the common language between these verses and the beginning of the chapter on the birth from the womb (Isa 49:1) suggests that it is the same Servant, also distinct from Israel, that is in view also there.

112

In fact, the shift from the Servant as Israel to the Servant as a distinct individual takes place right here from Isa 49.[6] Indeed, just two verses before in Isa 48:20 the Servant is explicitly identified as Jacob.

The same clear distinction between Israel and the Servant is found in Isa 50:10, where the prophet's appeal to Israel to "fear the Lord" parallels his call to "obey the voice of His Servant"; it follows that the Servant and the people of Israel are clearly two different entities:

Who among you [Israel][7] fears the Lord?

Who obeys the voice of His Servant?

It is already significant that the verses that just precede our text have depicted the Servant in clear distinction from Israel. An examination of the song of the Suffering Servant

---

6. The text of Isa 49:3 does not contradict our observation. Indeed the Masoretic accentuation of the text, which puts the greatest disjunctif *athnach* under the word "you" suggests that the Servant should be read disconnected from Israel, according to the following literal translation: "He [God] said to me: 'my Servant are you [*athnach*]; as far as Israel is concerned [anticipatory emphasis], it is in [through] you that I will glorify myself.'" Since God is addressing the Servant in the masculine second person singular "you" (*'atah*), it is logical that the other second person of the verse *bekha* "in you" also applies to the Servant and not to Israel. Verse 5 confirms this application since God's glorification is also there achieved through the Servant: "I shall be glorified [note the Niphal echoing the Hitpael of 'glorify' in v. 3] in the eyes of the Lord." In other words, as far as Israel is concerned (her salvation and destiny), God will glorify Himself through (in) the Servant (see the same use of the preposition *bekha* in Gen 12:3). It is through the Servant that God's glorification will take place in regards to the salvation of Israel; see Isa 44:23 and 60:21, where God's glorification (with the same Hebrew word *hitpa'er*) is associated with the salvation of Israel.

7. That the prophet addresses Israel is implied in the use of the second person plural that designates the people of Israel in our specific context (see Isa 50:1; 51:1–3).

is now necessary to verify to what extent the Suffering Servant is Israel or another entity distinct from it. For that matter, it is first important to be able to identify those who are implied in the first person plural ("we," "us," "our"). In other words, who are those who say in Isaiah 53:1: "Who has believed our report?" Are they Israel who are addressing the nations just mentioned above (Isa 52:10)? Or are they, on the contrary, those very nations who are speaking? This question is important for the identification of the Servant. Indeed, if the speaker is the nations, as it has sometimes been suggested,[8] it follows that the Servant could be Israel atoning for the sins of the nations. If, however, on the contrary, the speaker is Israel, it follows that the Servant could not be Israel, but someone else who would, then, atone for Israel and the nations.

2. The Use of the First Person Plural: Who Speaks?

A systematic investigation of the use of the first person plural in the book of Isaiah reveals that whenever the first person plural is used ("we," "us," "our," etc.), it always refers to Israel or Judah.[9] On the basis of these observations in our text

---

8. This traditional Jewish interpretation was given in the context of the Jewish-Christian polemic; see, for instance, Rashi (1040–1105), Ibn Ezra (1093–1168), Kimhi (1160–1235) in their commentaries in *Miqraoth Gedoloth* ad loc; for their translations, see A. Neubauer and S. R. Driver, *The Fifty-Third Chapter of Isaiah According to the Jewish Interpreters*, vol. 2 (New York: Ktav, 1969), 37–39, 43–48, 49–56; see also Karaite Rabbi Isaac ben Abraham of Troki (1525–1586) in Stephan Schreiner, "Isaiah 53 in the Book *Hizzuk Emunah* ('Faith strengthened') by Rabbi Isaac ben Abraham of Troki," in *The Suffering Servant, Isaiah 53 in Jewish and Christian Sources*, ed. Bernd Janowski and Peter Stuhlmacher (Grand Rapids, MI: Eerdmans, 2004), 418–449.

9. Isaiah 1:9; 9:10; 16:6; 22:13; 24:16; 25:9; 26:1, 8, 13, 17–18; 28:15; 33:2; 42:24; 59:9–12; 64:3, 5–6, 8–9.

and in the general context of the whole book, it is reasonable to conclude that the speakers in Isaiah 53 are the people of Israel, and by implication the listeners are the nations. The Servant is, therefore, someone distinct from Israel, as is evident from the following verses:

> When **we** [Israel] see Him [the Servant], there is no beauty that **we** [Israel] should desire Him [the Servant]. (53:2)

> And **we** [Israel] hid,[10] as it were, our faces from Him [the Servant]; . . . and **we** [Israel] did not esteem Him [the Servant]. (53:3)

> Surely He [the Servant] has borne **our** [Israel] griefs and carries **our** [Israel] sorrows; yet **we** [Israel] esteemed Him [the Servant] stricken. (53:4)

> But He [the Servant] was wounded for **our** [Israel] iniquities . . . the chastisement for **our** [Israel] peace was upon Him [the Servant], and by His [the Servant] stripes we [Israel] are healed. (53:5)

> All **we** [Israel] like sheep have gone astray; . . . and the Lord has laid on Him [the Servant] the iniquity of **us** [Israel] all. (53:6).

---

10. Note that the same motif of "hiding the face" also reappears in the next chapter in connection with Israel (54:8).

For the transgressions of My people[11] [Israel] He [the Servant] was stricken.[12] (53:8)

3. The Play on the Word *shama'*: Who hears?

It has been argued that the Suffering Servant can only be Israel since those who exclaim in wonder "who has believed our report?" (Isa 53:1) are identified as the kings and the nations referring to Israel as the Servant.[13] But the linguistic

---

11. The attribution of "transgressions" to "My people" clearly differentiates the people from the Servant, since the Servant is without transgression (see Isa 53:9). Some interpreters argue that the text refers here to the "peoples" (in the plural) to support the idea that this is Israel. But the Massoretic text has clearly the singular *'ammi* "my people," a reading supported by the Septuagint and the Targums; the speaker in the first person singular may be either the prophet or rather God Himself as it is in 53:11–12. The Qumran manuscript has *'ammo*, "his people," also in connection to God. This reading is also supported from within the text of Isaiah itself since the word "transgression" (*pesha'*) is always associated with Israel in the book of Isaiah (see 43:25; 44:22; 50:1; 58:1; 59:12, 20). Note that 58:1 associates the word "transgression" (*pesha'*) with the word *'ammi*, ("my people") also with God as the speaker, thus supporting the use of the same association in our text.

12. The Hebrew has *nega' lamo* which literally means "stricken for them." The word *nega'* should be understood as a Niphal (passive; cf. Josh 8:15) for the following reasons: (1) it parallels the word *nigzar* (cut off) which is in the Niphal form; (2) it has been so understood by the Septuagint version and the Qumran version (see *Biblia Hebraica Stuttgartensia* ad loc); (3) also the other occurrence of the word (53:4) comes with a passive sense in the passive participle form *nāgûa*. As for the pronominal suffix in *lamo* (for them), it refers back to the immediate antecedent, namely the collective "my people," to say that the Servant was stricken "for them." See also Gen 9:26–27; Deut 33:2; Isa 30:5; Ps 73:10; and E. Kautzsch, ed., *Gesenius' Hebrew Grammar*, rev. A. E. Cowley (Oxford: Clarendon Press, 1910), 103ff.

13. See for instance Rabbi Tovia Singer, "Kings of nations are speaking here in their numbed astonishment; for what they are finally witnessing is in stark contrast to everything they had ever heard or considered. Predictably, the first question on their lips will be, 'Who would have ever believed such thing?' They are utterly astounded that the Jewish people, whom all the nations have together despised and molested, are finally vindicated and enjoy the promise of salvation." (*Let's Get Biblical*, Study Guide [Monsey, NY: Outreach Judaism, 2001], 25).

link on *shama‘* ("hear") between the end of 52:15 and 53:1 suggests instead that those who speak cannot be the kings and the nations:

> What they [the kings and nations] had not heard [*sham‘u*]. (Isa 52:15)

> Who has believed our report [*shemu‘ah*]? (Isa 53:1)

The speakers of 53:1 who makes the "report" (*shemu‘ah*, past participle, literally means: "what is heard"), and says, "Who has believed our report?" cannot also be those who "hear" (*sham‘u*) this report in 52:15 (just plain logic).[14] Who then is the one making the report? The speaker, here, can only be Israel herself. This is confirmed by a similar situation in Isa 49:1 where Israel is clearly identified as the speaker (49:3); there also Israel invites the nations to "hear" (*shama‘*).

In this chapter, the Servant is clearly distinguished from the people of Israel; yet the Servant is related to Israel. This relationship between Israel and the Suffering Servant is so tight that they are both qualified with the same title, *‘ebed* "servant." The Servant is so close to Israel that He even identifies with His people Israel and goes so far as to take their place in order to save them. In fact, this relationship is suggested in the passage that precedes our text. In Isa 52:3–6, it is the suffering and "oppressed" condition of the people (vv. 4–5) that triggers God's action to "comfort" and "redeem" "his people" (vv. 6–9).

---

14. Cf. John Goldingay's comment on the identity of the "we" who speak: "It is hardly the nations and kings of 52:15, because they tell us that they had not heard the message, nor therefore had they delivered one." (*Isaiah*, New International Biblical Commentary [Peabody, MA: Hendrickson, 2001], 304).

It is now interesting to note that this divine redemption is qualified with the same language which describes the coming of the Suffering Servant; they both "disclose" the "arm of the Lord": "The Lord has made bare His holy arm" (52:10); "And to whom has the arm of the Lord been revealed?" (53:1). Furthermore both passages imply the presence and the testimony of the nations (52:10b; cf. 52:15). The parallels between these two passages reveal the nature of the relationship between the Servant and Israel. Identified as "the arm of the Lord," the Servant, distinct from Israel, is therefore, the one who will redeem and comfort the people of Israel.

The Servant as Atoning Sacrifice

The central idea of the passage is the suffering and dying of the Servant. Just in the English translation we count at least ten references to his suffering: "marred" (52:14), "despised" (53:3), "rejected" (53:3), "sorrows" (53:3, 4), "grief" (53:3, 10), "stricken" (53:4, 8), "afflicted" (53: 4), "wounded" (53:5), "bruised" (53:5, 10), "oppressed" (53:7). The death and even the burial of the Servant are explicitly mentioned: "they made His grave with the wicked but with the rich at His death"[15] (Isa 53:9).

15. The Hebrew word *bemutaw* (Isa 53:9) is in the plural, meaning literally, "his deaths," implying the death of several people, a meaning which would not make sense in our context. This strange plural form has led many commentators to emendate the word and read *bamato* ("his tomb") in the light of the Qumran Version (see *BHS* ad loc). There is no need, however, to emendate the word which may well be a plural of intensity to express the violent character of his death; the same plural form is applied to an individual, for instance, in Ezek 28:10, to qualify "the death of the slain" (Ezek 28:8, 9); cf. also Jer 16:4. The use of the plural form could also be explained as an end rhyme responding to the last word of the next phrase, *bepiw* ("in his mouth"); this poetic feature is well attested in biblical Hebrew and well used in Isaiah (see Wilfred G. E. Watson, *Traditional Techniques in Classical Hebrew Verse*, JSOT, Supplement [Sheffield: Sheffield Academic Press, 1994], 150, 172).

The main point, repeated over and over again is that this suffering and this death have an atoning purpose. This theme appears in eight out of the twelve verses (Isa 53:4–8, 10–12). It actually constitutes the middle section of the chiasm. Significantly the process of atonement is expressed and described with terms and motifs directly borrowed from the Levitical realm. The Servant is compared to a lamb ready for slaughter (Isa 53:7; cf. Gen 2:7; Lev 4:32; 5:6; 14:13, 21, etc.). The passive form, one of the most characteristic features of the Levitical style,[16] is most prominent in our passages. It is used sixteen times in the text; twelve of them[17] are in the Niphal, the technical form of the priestly "declaratory verdict" which is normally used in connection with sacrificial ritual. And this religious-cultic intention is further confirmed by the seven references to "sin," covering all three technical terms[18] (*pasha'*, *'awon*, *het'*):

v. 5: He was wounded for our transgressions [*pasha'*],

He was bruised for our iniquities [*'awon*];

v. 6: And the Lord has laid on Him the iniquities [*'awon*] of us all.

v. 11: He shall bear their iniquities [*'awon*].

v. 12: He bore the sin [*het'*] of many.

This language is quite familiar and suggests that the Servant is identified as the sacrificial offering which in the Levitical

---

16. See specifically the form *nislah* ("to be forgiven") in Lev 4:20, 26, 31, 35; 5:16; cf. also other verbs in Lev 7:20–21, 27; 13:7; cf. Gordon J. Wenham, *The Book of Leviticus* (Grand Rapids, MI: W. B. Eerdmans, 1979), 125, 241.

17. The four other forms are two in the Pual and two in the Hophal.

18. See Exod 34:7.

ON THE WAY TO EMMAUS

system was bearing the sin and hence permitted forgiveness from God: "If he brings a lamb as his sin offering, . . . he shall lay his hand on the head of the sin offering, . . . So the priest shall make atonement for his sin [*het'*] that he has committed, and it shall be forgiven him" (Lev 4:32–35).

The Servant as King

The identification of being a servant in itself often bears the implication of being of royal nature. Often Oriental kings were described as "servants" of their gods.[19] Indeed from the first words of the song, the Servant will consistently be described as a royal figure who shall "be exalted and extolled and be very high" (52:13); He is thus associated with kings who "shut their mouths at Him" (52:15) and with "the great" and "the strong" with whom he shares the same wealth (53:12). Also, the word "seed" (53:10) which is used to characterize His posterity indicates that this Servant belongs to the Davidic line, since the word "seed" is a technical word in the book of Isaiah to designate specifically Davidic posterity.[20] And, indeed, the very name given to Him, "My Servant" (*'abdi*) in the introduction (52:13) and in the conclusion (53:11) confirms this identification since this is one of the most frequent titles given in the Bible to King David.[21] And this title of King David is even attested in the book of Isaiah itself, where God calls him, "My Servant [*'abdi*] David" (Isa 37:34–35).

---

19. See Roland de Vaux, *The Bible and the Ancient Near East* (Garden City, NY: Doubleday, 1971), 155.

20. See Isa 41:8; 43:5; 44:3; 45:19, 25; 59:21; 61:9; 65:9; 66:22; cf. also Jer 31:36–37; 33:26; 2 Chr 20:7.

21. 2 Sam 3:18; 7:5; 1 Kgs 11:32, 36, 38; 14:8; 2 Kgs 19:34; 20:6; 1 Chr 17:7.

It is also significant that this divine association expressed through the expression "My Servant" (*'abdi*) is characteristic to the text of 2 Sam 7 where God sets up His eternal covenant with David. This formula is in fact used seven times[22] in this text as a rhetorical emphasis to underline the particular relationship between God and King David.

God as the Servant

As strange as it may appear, the Servant is identified with God Himself. This identification is so important and so significant that it is brought out repeatedly and in various ways through specific expressions in the Song of the Suffering Servant.

1. The High and Lofty One

The divine identity of the Servant is already affirmed from the very first words in the first verse of the song where the Servant is immediately presented as "extolled and very high" (Isa 52:13). This technical expression (in Hebrew: *rum wenisa'*) appears indeed only in two other verses of Isaiah to characterize God in His transcendence, referring to God's most sublime and holy presence in heaven:

> I saw the Lord sitting on a throne **high and lifted up**, and the train of His robe filled the temple. Above it stood seraphim; each one had six wings; with two he covered his face, with two he covered his feet, and with two he flew.

---

22. See 2 Sam 7:5, 8, 19, 20, 21, 25, 29.

And one cried to another and said:

"Holy, holy, holy is the Lord of hosts;

The whole earth is full of His glory." (Isa 6:1–3)

For thus says the **High and Lofty One**

Who inhabits eternity, whose name is Holy:

"I dwell in the high and holy place." (Isa 57:15)

When Isaiah is for the first time confronted to this divine vision, he is stunned: "Woe is me, for I am mute.[23] Because I am a man of unclean lips; and I dwell in the midst of a people of unclean lips; for my eyes have seen the King, the Lord of hosts" (Isa 6:5).

Significantly, those who are confronted to the vision of the Servant have the same reaction: "there were many who were appalled at Him" (Isa 52:14 NIV). The kings of the Song who are sharing the same vision "shut their mouths at Him" (Isa 52:15a); because what they hear and see is unheard of: "For what had not been told them they shall see, and what they had not heard they shall consider" (Isa 52:15b).

The only adequate human expression at this vision is therefore, besides the stunned silence, the question of wonder: "Who has believed our report?" (Isa 53:1). This is unbelievable! (Isa 52:14). Wonder at the fact that the One, so High, so Lofty, so Holy has come down so low: "a tender plant . . . a root out of dry ground" (Isa 53:2a), with "no form or comeliness . . . no beauty that we should desire Him" (Isa 53:2b), "despised and

---

23. The Hebrew word *nidmeiti*, usually translated "I am undone" or something similar, means literally "I was silent" (or "mute"), a translation that is supported by ancient Greek versions (the Septuagint: "stunned"; Symmachus, Aquilas and Theodotion: "I am silent"), the Latin Vulgate, and ancient Jewish exegesis. "The meaning 'be silent' has now been adopted very widely" (John W. Watts, *Isaiah*, Word Biblical Commentary, vol. 24 [Waco: TX: Word Books, 1985], 69, n. 5b).

rejected by men, a man of pains and familiar with suffering"[24] (Isa 53:3a), "despised and we did not esteem Him" (Isa 53:3c). Twice the word "man" is repeated in a row, "rejected of men, man of pains," responding to the two other references to "man" and "son of man" of 52:14. This play on the word "man" emphasizes the human condition of this transcendent Being— He is still of the same nature as those who reject Him—but his "human" condition is even worse than theirs, "so disfigured beyond that of any man, and His form marred beyond human likeness" (Isa 52:14).

2. The Hiding of Face

Another evidence for the identification of the Servant with God is implicitly given through the metaphor of the "hiding of face" (*seter panim*): "We hid, as it were, our faces from Him" (53:3). This is an important motif in the book of Isaiah. Of the 31 occurrences in the Bible,[25] eight are found in the book of Isaiah,[26] where this expression always involves a relationship between humans and God. One characteristic example occurs just a few verses after our passage, where God declares: "With a little wrath I hid My face from you for a moment" (Isa 54:8).

Except for Exod 3:6, where Moses "hides his face" before God,[27] all the biblical passages apply this expression to God as

---

24. Our translation of the Hebrew word *yada'*, which suggests more than the cognitive idea contained in the English word "acquainted" (NKJV), implies rather an experiential familiarity; see the NIV: "familiar with suffering."

25. Eleven in the Psalms (10:11; 22:25; 27:9; 30:8; 31:21; 51:11; 69:18; 88:15; 102:3; 104:29; 143:7), 3 in Job (13:10; 24:15; 34:29), 3 in Deuteronomy (31:17, 18; 32:20), 1 in Jeremiah (33:5) and 2 in Ezekiel (39:23, 24), 1 in Micah (3:4).

26. Isaiah 8:17; 50:6; 53:3; 54:8; 59:2; 64:6. (45:15 and 57:17 use only the abbreviated expression "hide," without the word "face").

27. Genesis 3:8 has another verb for "hiding" *hithabe'*, which appears, however, here also in association with the face (*panim*) of God.

the subject. It is God who hides His face. The Prophet Isaiah goes so far as to make the "hiding of face" a distinctive feature of the relationship between Israel and the true God. It is clear, then, from the use of the expression *seter panim* "hiding of face" in the Bible that, whether God is the subject of the verb (the majority of the cases) or the object of the verb (two cases), He is the One from whom humans hide their face; this expression always appears in connection to God:

> God hides His face before humans (the majority of cases)
>
> Humans (Moses, we) hide their face before God (Exod 3:6; Isa 53:3).

Since the expression "hiding of face" is used in Isa 53:3 with "we" (humans) as a subject, the object of the verb, the Suffering Servant, could well be identified with God Himself.[28]

Now, the fact that this particular expression *seter panim* ("hiding of face") appears here in the middle of the paragraph of v. 3, in the center, the apex of the chiasm, is indicative of the intention to suggest the significance and centrality of its message:[29]

> A despised and rejected by men, a man of pains and familiar with suffering,
>
> **B we hid our faces [*seter panim*] from Him;**
>
> A¹ despised and we did not esteem Him. Surely He has borne our suffering and carried our pains.[30]

---

28. It is interesting that the same figure of a humiliated Suffering Servant is given in Isa 50:6, as the subject of the verb "hiding of face."

29. R. L. Alden, "Is the High Point of a Psalm's Chiasmus the Point of the Psalm?" A paper read at the Society of Biblical Literature Annual Meeting, Chicago, November 1988.

30. Our translation takes into consideration the use of the same Hebrew words (*ka'av* and *choli*) in A and A¹, namely "pains" and "suffering."

The chiasm A B A¹, makes A¹ respond to A, using the same Hebrew words and corresponding motifs in parallelism, and places B, the *seter panim,* in the center, a way to express the author's wonder that it is God who is hiding there, in the "despised," the "pains," the disease and the inhuman figure, the last place indeed where God would be expected to be.

3. Universal Scope

The Servant's domain affects "many nations" and "kings" (52:15). The word *rabbim* ("many"), which is repeated five times in our texts (52:14, 15; 53:11, 12a, 12b), is a technical term often used in the Bible to cover a universal scope (see especially Dan 9:27; 11:33; 12:4, etc.). Also, the divine quality of the Servant is suggested in the fact that He is able to "justify many" (53:11), a qualification which belongs to the judge (Deut 25:1) or to God himself (1 Kgs 8:32).

It is significant that v. 6, which constitutes the center of the Song, is literally framed in an *inclusio* with the Hebrew word *kol* ("all"). This is the word that is traditionally used to express the universal reference. It is the key word, for instance, of the passage marking the end of the Creation story (Gen 2:1–3), where it is used three times to refer to the cosmos, the whole creation of God. In our passage, the "all" applies to the people who are speaking: "all of us" (*kullanu*). The first "all of us" concerns the erring of the people, "all we [*kullanu*] like sheep have gone astray." The second "all of us" concerns the iniquity of the people: "And the Lord has laid on Him the iniquity of us all" (*kullanu*). Beyond the people of Israel, it is the whole humankind that is embraced, a universal scope that implies the presence and the involvement of the God Creator of the universe.

Isaiah 53 in the Hebrew Bible

Isaiah 7:14

The thematic parallels in contrast, which have been pointed out in the introduction between the context surrounding the birth of Immanuel and the context surrounding the death of the Suffering Servant, suggest some kind of relation between the two events. Furthermore, these parallels are reinforced by the observation of common motifs and linguistic links between Isa 7:14 and the first introduction of the Servant in Isa 49:1, 5 (in bold in the quoted verses below). Thus we note the common evocations of "mother," conception in her womb, divine calling of the name, and the use of the same words: *shim'u* "listen" (Isa 7:13, cf. Isa 49:1), *qara'* "call" (Isa 7:14, cf. Isa 49:1), and *shem* "name" (Isa 7:14, cf. Isa 49):

> Then He [the Lord] **said**, "**Hear** . . . **The Lord** Himself . . . Behold, the virgin shall **conceive and bear a son** and **call** His **name** Immanuel." (Isa 7:13–14)

> **Listen** . . . **The Lord** has **called** me from the **womb, from the matrix of my mother** He has **made mention** of my **name**. (Isa 49:1)

> And now the **Lord says**, who formed me from the **womb** to be His Servant. (Isa 49:5)

The parallels between the two verses (Isa 49:1, 5) suggest that the text refers to the same Servant, that is the one who is distinct from Israel, and more precisely the one who receives the mission to "bring Jacob back to Him [God] . . . raise up the tribes of Jacob . . . be My salvation [God's] to the ends of the earth" (Isa 49:5–6). This description of the Servant's mission clearly excludes Israel, since he is presented in contradistinction from Jacob and Israel, as well as the prophet Isaiah,[31] since the fulfillment of that prophecy, the return from Babylon (Isa 48:20), still belongs to a far future beyond the time of Isaiah. On the other hand, Isa 49 identifies the Servant in terms that strikingly remind of the Suffering Servant as portrayed in the fourth Servant song:

> In the shadow of His hand He has **hidden** [*str*] Me . . . In His quiver He has **hidden** [*str*] Me. (Isa 49:2)

> Him whom man **despises** [*bzh*], to him whom the nation abhors, to the Servant of rulers: Kings shall **see** [*r'h*] and arise. Princes also shall worship. (Isa 49:7).

> **Kings** shall shut their mouths at Him; for what had not been told them they shall **see** [*r'h*], and what they have not heard they shall consider. (Isa 52:15)

> When we **see** [*r'h*] Him there is no beauty that we should desire Him. He is **despised** [*bzh*] and rejected by men, a man of sorrows . . . and we **hid** [*str*], as it were, our faces from Him, He was **despised** [*bzh*] and we did not esteem Him. (Isa 52:15–53:2–3)

Beyond the literary implications in regard to the unity of the book of Isaiah these parallels between the two texts suggest an interesting connection between the two figures.[32] Would the

31. Contra Goldingay, 281–282.

32. On a possible literary connection between the book of Immanuel (Isa 7–12) and the book of the Suffering Servant (Isa 49–55), see Richard M. Davidson, "The Messianic Hope in Isaiah 7:14 and the Volume of Immanuel (Isaiah 7–12)," in *"For You Have Strengthened Me": Biblical and Theological Studies in Honor of Gerhard Pfandl in Celebration of His Sixty-Fifth Birthday*, ed. Martin Pröbstle with assistance of Gerald A. Klingbeil and Martin G. Klingbeil (St. Peter am Hart, Austria: Seminar Schloss Bogenhofen, 2007). 95.

child Immanuel born from a virgin be the same person as the Suffering Servant?

Isaiah 43:24

The same idea of God suffering because of the iniquities of His people (Isa 53:5–6) is also found in Isa 43:24: "But you have burdened Me with your sins, you have wearied Me with your iniquities." That the two passages are connected is further confirmed on the level of language. It is noteworthy, indeed, that both passages share the same association of the three technical words for sin (*het'*, "sin," v. 24b; *'awon*, "iniquity," v. 24c; *pasha'* "transgression," v. 25). Both passages are related to the sacrificial rites. In 53:7, we have the word *seh* ("lamb") and *zebah* ("sacrifice"); in 43:23–24, we have also the word *seh* ("lamb") and *tebah* ("slaughter"). Furthermore, it is no accident that the key word of 43:24 is *'abad* (here translated "burdened") from which the word for "servant" is derived. A literal translation of this verse would thus read: "But you have made Me a servant [*'abad*] with your sins" (Isa 43:24).

It is interesting that in Isa 43:24b the verb *'abad* echoes another occurrence of *'abad* in Isa 43:23, where it is used in relation to the sacrificial offering. These verses should then be rendered according to the following: "I have not made you a servant through sacrifice . . ." (Isa 43:23); "But you have made Me a servant through your sins" (Isa 43:24). The mystery of the Suffering Servant in Isa 53 is then decoded. His identity is revealed: it is God Himself. The reason why He is called a Servant is given: because of the sins of the people. And the means through which the broken relationship between God and His people will be restored and divine forgiveness granted is shown: not merely through the usual Levitical sacrifice, but through God Himself; God Himself functions as the sacrifice: "Nor have you honored Me with your sacrifices. I have not caused you to serve with grain offerings, . . . nor have you satisfied Me with the fat of your sacrifices: . . . I, even I, am He who blots out your transgressions for My own sake" (Isa 43:23–25).

Psalm 22

Outside the book of Isaiah, the biblical text, which echoes Isa 53 the most, is Ps 22. Not only specific motifs or ideas but also particular words and expressions are shared by these two passages.

The general common motif is the suffering of the righteous man. In both passages the victim is humiliated and despised by men (Isa 53:3, 7; cf. Ps 22:6; Heb. v. 7); and the common words between the two passages are *bzh* ("despised") and *'anah* ("afflicted"/"humiliated"). In both texts the victim is apparently abandoned by God (Isa 53:4; cf. Ps 22:8; Heb. v. 9) and is the object of oppression (Isa 53:7; cf. Ps 22:16; Heb., v. 17).

It is noteworthy that we find in both passages, within the same context of humiliation and suffering (Isa 53:3–4; cf. Ps 22:24; Heb. v. 25), the same expression *seter panim mimmennu* ("hide one's face from him"), and in Ps 22 the expression is clearly applied to God. The close relation between the two expressions used within the same association of words and thoughts allows for a connected reading between the two passages and confirms that in Isa 53:3 it is God who is implied as the subject of the hiding of the face.

Another important common element between the two passages concerns their strong universal perspective. Isa

53 closes with a threefold reference to the salvation of the nations (vv. 11–12). The Hebrew word *rabbim* ("many") is repeated three times, echoing the *goyim rabbim* ("many nations") of the introduction of the poem (Isa 52:15) in an inclusio. Likewise, Ps 22 concludes with a beautiful chiasm by a four-fold reference to the salvation of the nations. The Hebrew word *kol* ("all") is repeated four times (Ps 22:27–29; Heb. vv. 28–30) and explicitly related to the nations of the world: "all the ends of the world" (v. 27a; Heb. 28a); "all the families of the nations" (v. 27b; Heb. 28b); "all the prosperous of the earth" (v. 29; Heb. 30); "all those who go down to the dust." It is noteworthy that this echo of rhythm and ideas is also accompanied by the use of common wording. In both passages, we find the same association of the words: "posterity" (*zera'*), "serve" (*'abad*), "righteousness" (*tsedeq*) (Ps 22:30–31; cf. Isa 53:10–11).

Daniel 12:1–3

The passage on resurrection in Dan 12:1–3 alludes to the song of the Suffering Servant through a number of linguistic links:

> *haskil* (Dan 12:3a; cf. Isa 52:13)

> *hatsdiq* (Dan 12:3b; cf. Isa 53:11)

> *rabbim* (Dan 12:2, 3b; cf. Isa 52:14, 15; 53:11, 12)

From this clear echo between the two texts, it could be inferred that the author of Dan 12 has understood the text of the Suffering Servant in a messianic and eschatological sense, even supporting the interpretation of the resurrection of the Suffering Servant in the difficult verse of Isa 53:10a.[33]

All these thematic, structural, and linguistic coincidences cannot be accidental. They suggest that the same messianic figure is implied in both texts.[34] The messianic interpretation of Isa 53 is then supported not only on the basis of other passages in the book of Isaiah, but also from the broader testimony of the Hebrew Bible.

Summary

The portrait of the Suffering Servant displays a multifaceted figure. A number of clues collected in the Song of Isaiah 52:13–53:12 and in its related texts suggest the following features for the Servant:

---

33. See H. L. Ginsburg, "The Oldest Interpretation of the Suffering Servant" *Vetus Testamentum* 3 (1953): 402. This allusion does not mean, however, that Daniel identifies the *masqilim* with the Suffering Servant (see Ginsberg, ibid.). It simply suggests that the *masqilim* will share the same destiny as the Servant: both will resurrect. Likewise, the parallels and the linguistic links, which may be observed between the verse describing the standing up of Michael (Dan 12:1a and the verse describing the resurrection of the righteous in Dan 12:1b–2a does not mean that Michael should be identified with the righteous people; just as the echo between the standing up of Daniel *'md* (Dan 12:13), and the standing up (*'md*) of Michael (Dan 12:1), does not mean that Daniel is to be identified as Michael; (on these connections, see Jacques Doukhan, "From Dust to Stars: The Vision of Resurrection(s) in Daniel 12,1–3 and Its Resonance in the Book of Daniel," paper presented at the Resurrection of the Dead: Biblical Traditions in Dialogue International Symposium, Louvain-la-Neuve, Belgium, 8 April 2010.). The same reasoning holds in regard to the echoes between the text of the Suffering Servant in Isa 53 and the other servant Israel. These particular connections have rather to do with the Hebrew view of corporate personality, which likes to identify the individual with the group (see H. Wheeler Robinson, *Corporate Personality in Ancient Israel* [Philadelphia, PA: Fortress Press, 1980]).

34. The Jewish messianic interpretation of Ps 22 is found especially in the Midrashim (see *Pesiqta Rabbati*, Pis 37, Isaiah 61:10; see also *Midrash Tehilim*, Psalm 22:1).

1. **Distinct entity from Israel**: the Servant is identified as the Redeemer/gatherer of Israel (Isa 49:5–7), the One whom Israel obeys (Isa 50:10), and therefore cannot be Israel; Israel is the speaker "we" (Isa 1:1 ff.) for whom the Servant will atone (esp. Isa 53:4–6) and therefore cannot be the Servant.

2. **Davidic king**: the Servant is associated with kings (Isa 52:15; 53:12); the Servant is called "My Servant," as king David is called (Isa 52:12; 53:11; cf. 37:35; 2 Sam 7) and is associated with the "seed" (*zera'*)—a motif that is characteristic to the messianic Davidic line (Isa 53:10, cf. 41:8, etc.).

3. **Transcendent God**: the Servant is qualified as "High and Lofty," a title that is only used to evoke the High and Holy God who sits on the throne in heaven (Isa 52:13; cf 6:1–3; 57:15); the Servant relates to humans through the category of the hidden face *seter panim* (Isa 53:3), a dimension that is exclusive to the divine-human encounter (Isa 54:8; Ps 22:24, etc.); the Servant is identified as the Lord's arm (Isa 50:10); the Servant is Universal, affecting the "many" (Isa 52:14; 53:11, 12), the "nations" (Isa 52:15), and "all of us" (Isa 53:6). God Himself identifies Himself as the Servant for the sake of the sins of Israel (Isa 43:24).

4. **Sacrifice**: The Servant is equated with a sacrificial animal as suggested through the comparison to lamb led to slaughter (Isa 53:7) and the rich sacrificial language and the intertextual connection of the Suffering Servant Song with Isa 43:24 and Ps 22. The literary construction, which places the theme of atonement in the middle of the chiasm (Isa 53:4–6), testifies to the importance of this sacrificial function of the Servant.

Isaiah 53 in Jewish Tradition

Qumran

The messianic interpretation of Isa 53 is already found as early as the second century B.C.E. in the Qumran community that applied the prophecy of Isa 53 to the "Savior Messiah."[35] A powerful illustration of this application is found in the so-called "self-glorification hymn," written in the first century B.C.E., where the text of Isa 53 is quoted (in italics in the following text), and applied to a non-identified messianic figure:

El 'Elyon gave me a seat among the perfect ones of [. . . et]ernal;

A mighty throne in the congregation of the gods

Above which none of the kings of the East shall sit
. . .

My glory is in[comparable]

And besides me no-one is exalted, nor comes to me,

I reside in [. . .] heavens . . .

I am counted among the gods

And my dwelling is in the holy congregation . . .

Who has been considered despicable on my account?

---

35. See André Dupont-Sommer, *The Essene Writings from Qumran*, trans. G. Vermes (Gloucester, MA : Peter Smith, 1973), 364–366.

. . .

Who bea[rs] all sorrows like me? . . .

[. . . friend of the king, companion of the holy ones
. . . incomparable,

F]or among the gods is [my] position,

And my glory is with the sons of the king. (4Q491c
Self Glorification Hymn)[36]

Then the text continues in an additional hymn, which
contains this time, the word "Messiah":

[exult,] just ones, in the God of [. . .] in the holy
dwelling

sing for h[im] . . .
    to establish, the horn of [his] Messiah.[37]

Actually, the Qumran copy of the Suffering Servant Song
testifies to the messianic interpretation of that passage, since
the Servant is there identified as being anointed by God,
"messiah":

Just as many were astonished at you,

So I have anointed [*mashahti*][38] his appearance
beyond that of any [other] man.

---

36. See Bernd Janowski and Peter Stuhlmacher, eds, *The Suffering Servant,
Isaiah 53 in Jewish and Christian Sources* (Grand Rapids, MI: Eerdmans, 2004),
142–143.

37. Ibid., 143.

38. We note that the Qumran text has changed the Masoretic Text which has
instead *mishhat* or *mashhat*, meaning "marring," "disfigurement."

And his form beyond that of the sons of humanity.
(Isa 52:14, 1QIsaᵃ)

A second change of the Qumran text concerns vv. 53:5 and
10 where the Messiah is described as "pierced":

The Lord was pleased to crush him, He pierced him.
(Isa 53:5, 1QIsaᵃ)

But he was pierced through our transgressions. (Isa
53:10, 1QIsaᵃ)[39]

Another important variant that the Qumran Scroll brings
out is the addition of the word "light" in Isa 53:11:

Out of the suffering of his soul he will see *light*,

and find satisfaction. (Isa 53:11, 1QIsaᵃ)[40]

This last variant is particularly interesting as this reference
to "seeing" light follows the reference to his death (v. 9) and to
the fact that "he will see his seed" (v. 10), thus suggesting the
idea of life out of death, hence of his resurrection.

Talmud

A passage in the Talmud alludes to an old tradition
according to which, because of Isa 53:4, the Messiah was to
call himself a leper:

The masters [*Rabbana*] have said that the leper of the
school of the Rabbi . . . is his name, for it has been
said: "He has borne our diseases and he has borne our

---

39. Ibid., 105.
40. Ibid., 102.

sufferings, and we have considered him as a leper, smitten by God and humbled." (*Sanhedrin* 98b)[41]

Midrash

A characteristic invocation in the Midrash identifies the Suffering Servant as the Messiah:

> Messiah of our justice [*Meshiah Tsidkenu*], though we are Thy forebears, Thou art greater than we because Thou didst bear the burden of our children's sins, and our great oppressions have fallen upon Thee . . . Among the peoples of the world Thou didst bring only derision and mockery to Israel. . . . Thy skin did shrink, and Thy body did become dry as wood; Thine eyes were hollowed by fasting, and Thy strength became like fragmented pottery-all that came to pass because of the sins of our children. (*Pesiqta Rabbati, Pisqa* 37)

It is always the figure of the Suffering Messiah that *Midrash Rabbah* depicts as interceding for the sins of Israel:

> The Messiah King . . . will offer his heart to implore mercy and longsuffering for Israel, weeping and suffering as is written in Isaiah 53:5 "He was wounded for our transgressions," etc: when the Israelites sin, he invokes upon them mercy, as it is

---

41. The theological connection between the ritual of the sacrifice and the Messiah, which lies in the heart of Isa 53 is also attested in the Talmud. In fact, the whole sacrificial system was interpreted there as a reference to messianic hope: "R. Eleazar said in the name of R. Josei: 'This is a *halakha* [a principle] that concerns the Messiah.' Abba answered him: 'It is not necessary to give instructions here on all the sacrifices of victims, for this is a *halakha* that concerns the messianic era'" (*Zebahim* 44b and *Sanhedrin* 51b).

written: "Upon him was the chastisement that made us whole, and likewise the Lord has laid on him the iniquity of us all." And this is what the Holy One— let him be blessed forever!—decreed in order to save Israel and rejoice with Israel on the day of the resurrection. (*Bereshit Rabbati* on Genesis 24:67)

Speaking about the Messiah, another Midrash recognizes His transcendent superiority on the basis of Isa 52:13:

"Who are you, O great mountain?" . . . This refers to the King Messiah. And why is He called "great mountain?" Because He is greater than the patriarchs, as it is written in Isaiah 52:13, "Behold my Servant shall deal prudently, He shall be exalted and extolled and be very high." He will be more "exalted" than Abraham, more "extolled" than Moses and more "high" than the ministering angels. (*Tanhuma* on Genesis 27:30)[42]

The Targum

The Aramaic Targum of Jonathan also interprets Isa 53 in a messianic sense. Beginning with the introductory passages, the identity of the Servant is made clear:

Behold, my Servant the Messiah will prosper, be lifted up and made strong; so long did the house of Israel languish after him. (*Targum* on Isaiah 52:13)

---

42. Cf. *Yalkut Shimoni* 476.

Parallel Texts of Isaiah 53 Recognized as Messianic in Jewish Tradition

Speaking about the suffering of the Messiah the Midrash refers to **Psalm 22** as a support:

> It was taught that in the week when the Son of David will come, bars of stone will be brought and put on his neck until his body bends and he cries and weeps, and his voice rises. He will, then, speak to the face of the Lord of the world [God]: "how much will be my strength, and how much will be my breath and how much will be my soul, and how much will be my members? Am I not flesh and blood?" It is about this very hour that David had wept and had said, "my strength is dried up like a potsherd, and my tongue clings to my jaws" (Ps 22:15, Heb. 16). Then the Holy Be He [God] said to him . . . "that your pain be like mine". . . Then the Messiah answered to the Lord of the world: "now, my mind is appeased, it is enough for the servant to be like his master." (*Pesiqta Rabbati 36. Isaiah 60:1,2*, cf. *37. Isaiah 60:10*)

As documented by these texts, the early Jewish tradition regarding Isa 53 was clearly and strongly messianic. It is only later in the wake of the Jewish-Christian controversy that the identification of the Suffering Servant as the Messiah was considered as suspect and eventually abandoned. It is interesting, however, that in spite of the controversy some rabbis hold onto the traditional interpretation, as R. Moshe ben Nachman (Nachmanides, 13th century) testifies:

138

The right view . . . is to suppose that by the phrase "my Servant" the whole of Israel is meant . . . A different opinion, however, is adopted by the Midrash, which refers it to the Messiah, it is necessary for us to explain it in conformity with the view there maintained. The prophet says, the Messiah, the son of David of whom the text speaks . . . by His stripes we were healed because the stripes by which He is vexed and distressed will heal us; God will pardon us for His righteousness, and we shall be healed both for our own transgressions and from the iniquities of our fathers.[43]

More recently, a significant number of Orthodox Jews, the Lubavitch Hasidim, have applied the "Suffering Servant" of Isa 53 to their spiritual leader, the Rebbe, Menahem Mendel Schneerson (1902–1994). Obviously, the messianic identity of the Rebbe was not established, and he was not recognized as the Messiah by the majority of contemporary Jews. It is remarkable, though, that in spite of the old Jewish-Christian dispute, many Orthodox Jews still chose to resort to Isa 53 in their messianic argument; this shows how deep and strong and even authentic the messianic significance of this passage is in traditional Jewish consciousness.[44]

43. S. R. Driver and A. Neubauer, eds, *The Fifty-Third Chapter of Isaiah According to the Jewish Interpreters*, vol. 2 (New York: Ktav, 1969), 78.

44. See David Berger, *The Rebbe, the Messiah, and the Scandal of Orthodox Indifference* (Portland, OR: Littman Library of Jewish Civilization, 2001), 23.

Isaiah 53 in the New Testament

In the New Testament, the text of the Suffering Servant has been alluded to or quoted and explicitly applied to the Messiah.

Philippians 2:9

After having identified the Messiah as "a servant," a clear allusion to our text, the author of the epistle points to Isa 52:13 to affirm the transcendence of the Messiah:

> Therefore God also has highly exalted Him and given Him the name which is above every name.

Romans 15:21

The author of the epistle refers to Isa 52:15 to speak about the communication of the Gospel to the Gentiles:

> But as it is written: "To whom He was not announced, they shall see; and those who have not heard shall understand."

Matthew 8:17

The Evangelist applies Isa 53:4 to the healing work of the Messiah:

> He cast out the spirits with a word, and healed all who were sick, that it might be fulfilled which was spoken by Isaiah the prophet, saying: "He Himself took our infirmities and bore our sicknesses."

Acts 8:32–35

The Ethiopian eunuch was reading Isa 53:7-8 when he met Philip the apostle who explained to him that this passage concerned the Messiah:

THE SERVANT

The place in the Scripture which he read was this: "He was led as a sheep to the slaughter; and like a lamb silent before its shearer, so He opened not His mouth. In His humiliation His justice was taken away. And who will declare His generation? For His life is taken from the earth." So the eunuch answered Philip and said, "I ask you, of whom does the prophet say this, of himself or of some other man?" Then Philip opened his mouth, and beginning at this Scripture, preached Jesus to him.

1 Peter 2:21–22

Peter applied Isa 53:9 to the suffering of the Messiah:

For this you were called because Christ [Messiah] also suffered for us . . . "Who committed no sin, nor was guile found in His mouth."

The Messianic Suffering

The messianic suffering does not make sense. The absurd character of the Messiah's suffering has been captured in one of the most moving and at the same time most significant of all Messiah legends: despised and rejected by everyone the Messiah sits in the gates of Rome and forever winds and unwinds the bandages of his festering wounds,[45] and the Midrash comments: "pains have adopted him."[46] Indeed suffering is the most pervasive theme in the Servant Song.

---

45. *B. Sanhedrin* 98a.
46. *Sefer Zerubabel* (in Adolph Jellinek, *Bet haMidrash* [Jerusalem: Bamberger & Wahrman, 1938], 2:54–55).

It is not only evoked poetically through powerful images suggesting humiliation, "servant" (Isa 52:13); fragility, "tender plant"[47] (Isa 53:2); "despised" (Isa 53:2, 3); "rejected" (Isa 53:3); "sorrows" (Isa 53:3, 4); and victim, "lamb" (Isa 53:7), but also explicitly stated through an abundant vocabulary denoting suffering: "griefs" (Isa 53:4, 10); "stricken" (Isa 53:4, 8); "smitten" (Isa 53:4); "afflicted" (Isa 53:4, 7); "wounded" (Isa 53:55); "bruised" (Isa 53:5, 10); "stripes" (Isa 53:5); "oppressed" (Isa 53:7). The Servant is so related to suffering that he is even identified with it: He is "the man of suffering" (Isa 53:3). Suffering makes his identity.

Strangely, in the book of Isaiah, suffering is also identified with God Himself. Suffering is an inherent part of God's very nature; it is associated with His Holiness[48]:

> They grieved ['atsab] His holy [qadosh] spirit [ruach]. (Isa 63:10)

> The Holy One [qadosh] of Israel . . . The Lord has called you . . . grieved ['atsab] in spirit [ruach]. (Isa 54:5–6).

> You caused me to be servant ['bd][49] with your sins

> You caused me to suffer ['atsab] with your iniquities. (Isa 43:24, literal translation)

---

47. The Hebrew word *yoneq* refers to a suckling and fragile infant (Lam 2:11), "victim of hunger and thirst" (Helmer Ringgren, "*yoneq*," in *Theological Dictionary of the Old Testament*, ed. G. Johannes Botterweck and Helmer Ringgren [Grand Rapids, MI: Eerdmans, 1974], 6:108).

48. As Terence E. Fretheim comments: "It is not considered in the least incongruous to juxtapose grieving and holiness: it is God in all his Godliness who grieves," (*The Suffering of God* [Philadelphia: Fortress Press, 1984], 111).

49. The Hebrew verb *'avad* "serve" is here in the causative form (Hifil) and is translated with "burdened" by NKJV.

The parallel between the suffering of God and the suffering of the Servant is striking to the point where God is in Isa 43:24 identified with the Servant himself. They both suffer because of human sin, and they both suffer for the sake of forgiveness and salvation. It is significant that immediately after mentioning God's suffering because of the sins of Israel in Isa 43:24, v. 25 specifies that God forgives their sins:

> I, even I, am He who blots out your transgressions
> for My own sake;
>
> and I will not remember your sins.

This association of God's forgiveness with God's suffering clearly suggests some kind of relationship between God's suffering and God's forgiveness. This connection is in fact explicitly given in Isa 53 where we find the same three technical words for "sins."[50] There the servant is said to have been "wounded for our transgressions," "bruised for our iniquities," and "stricken" (Isa 53:5) for the transgressions of God's people (Isa 53:8). By the end of the song the same thought is expressed in other words. The servant "shall bear their iniquities" (Isa 53:11) and "the sin of many"(Isa 53:12). In the last two passages the choice of the words for "bear" (*sbl*, *ns'a*), respectively before "iniquities" and "sins," is particularly interesting as they are often used to denote "forgive" (Hos 1:6; 14:2). "To bear the sins" means "to forgive." Thus Isa 53 clearly echoes Isa 43:24–25.

There is just one slight difference between the two passages. In Isa 43:24–25, God is the subject of the verbs. He is the One

---

50. Both passages contain the words "sin" (*het'*), "iniquity" (*'awon*), "transgression" (*pesha'*); see Isa 43:24–25, cf. Isa 53:5, 8, and esp. 11–12.

who suffers and forgives the sins. In Isa 53, it is the Servant. Yet God is effectively present there also. This suffering for forgiveness by the Servant is explicitly claimed to be the will of God (Isa 53:4, 6, 10). This clear identification of the Lord as being the One who is behind the whole scenario, just as He is also the One who endures it, being both the subject and the object of the plan is confusing. Is the subject (God) "hiding" in the object (the Suffering Servant)? How could the Lord be there? How could God, the Creator, the eternal God of life, suffer and even die? This suffering of God for forgiveness does not make sense.

The image of the "hiding of face" that is used in this context explains, or at least suggests the mechanism of this difficult scenario of the humiliating of God, of His death. This "hiding of face" does not mean God's death or ours, and hence our separation from Him, but on the contrary it is a hiding that saves and paradoxically restores God's relationship with sinful humans. Significantly, this particular divine feature is contrasted to the idols. For the idols are seen unlike this God whose face is hidden:

> Truly You are God, who hide Yourself, O God of Israel the Savior!
>
> They shall be ashamed . . . They shall go in confusion together, who are makers of idols. (Isa 45:15–16).

Our verse makes it clear that, in contrast to the idols, the God who hides Himself is the true God, "the Savior." The next verse emphasizes the contrast. Immediately after mentioning the shame and confusion of the makers of idols in v. 16, v. 17 refers to the salvation of Israel by the Lord, the Creator:

> But Israel shall be saved by the Lord with an
> everlasting salvation; . . . the Lord who created the
> heavens, who is God, who formed the earth and
> made it. (Isa 45:17–18)

It is significant that salvation is related to these two dimensions of God's relationship with humans, namely the "hiding of the face" and the Lord who created. Salvation does not come from the idols one makes and sees, but from the Creator, the God one does not make and does not see. The process of salvation is thus suggested these two dimensions. Only the God one cannot see, who transcends human apprehension, the God who creates and who is therefore beyond human control is capable to save. This whole scenario of salvation goes then against common sense and natural expectation, a disturbing experience that resonates even in the words of those who are confronted with the Servant: "we esteemed . . . But in fact" (Isa 53:4–5).

The success of God's enterprise is thus related to the hiding of God's face behind the crushing of the Servant. Likewise for the Servant the offering of his life ("soul") for sin, which means His death, results in the seeing of the seed and the prolonging of days. The next verse (Isa 53:11) further develops this theme: the travail of the soul and His experience of suffering shall lead to the justification of many. The crushing and the death of the Servant not only leads to His survival out of death— He sees His seed (or if we follow the Qumran version, "He sees light")[51]—but also to the salvation of the world: "He shall

---

51. See Martin Hengel, "The Effective History of Isaiah 53 in the Pre-Christian Period," in *The Suffering Servant: Isaiah 53 in Jewish and Christian Sources*, ed. Bernd Janowski and Peter Stuhlmacher (Grand Rapids, MI: Eerdmanns, 2004), 102.

justify many." The echo on the words "soul" and "many" in v. 12 confirms that interpretation, since the death of the Servant means here the forgiveness of the sins of many, and therefore their justification and hence their salvation:

> Because He poured out His soul unto death . . . He bore the sin of many (Isa 53:12).

Unexpectedly, the positive emerges from the negative, just as the victory over death is gained through the death of the Seed (Gen 3:15), just as the Star emerges from the dust (Num 24:17), just as the birth germinates from the virgin (Isa 7:14). The repetition of this process shows its significance. Likewise in Isa 53, success rises from failure, which is here the despised, humiliated, suffering, and dead Servant. Verse 10 accounts to that paradox through the play of an *inclusio* that frames it; the verse begins and ends with the same words expressing the pleasure of the Lord:

> It **pleased** the Lord to bruise Him . . .

> The **pleasure** of the Lord shall prosper in His hand.

Obviously, God's hiding face in Isa 53 is not referring to a mere existential experience of all times or of all humans, or even to a dramatic event of immense proportions.[52] For sure

---

52. On the various Post-Holocaust readings of Isa 53 and its application to the event of the Holocaust or to other existential experiences of "God's hidden face," see my discussion in Jacques Doukhan, "Reading the Bible after Auschwitz," in *Remembering For the Future, The Holocaust in an Age of Genocide*, ed. John K. Roth and Elisabeth Maxwell (New York: Palgrave, 2001), 2:690–691; cf. Irving Greenberg, "Cloud of Smoke, Pillar of Fire," in *Holocaust, Religious & Philosophical Implications*, ed. John K. Roth and Michael Berenbaum (New York: Paragon House, 1989), 326–328.

these existential applications should not be excluded, for that story contains many valuable lessons of universal relevancy; yet these readings of the text should not miss or dismiss its primary intention, namely that it refers to an event that pertains to the divine domain. This is why this story remains for the essential beyond our human comprehension. Although we have understood how suffering is the key for the Servant's relationship with us, and although we have understood that the Servant suffers, *because of* our sins, and *in order to* forgive, we are still wondering about the sense of that suffering. But does not this wondering again testify to the hiding of the face?

CHAPTER V

THE SEVENS

Seventy weeks are determined for your people
and your holy city,
To finish the transgression,
To make an end of sins,
To make reconciliation for iniquity,
To bring in everlasting righteousness,
To seal up vision and prophecy,
And to anoint the Most Holy.
Know therefore and understand,
that from the going forth of the command to restore and
build Jerusalem until Messiah the Prince,
there shall be seven weeks and sixty two weeks;
The street shall be built again, and the wall,
even in troublesome times.
And after the sixty-two weeks the Messiah shall be cut off,
but not for Himself
And the people of the prince who is to come shall destroy
the city and the sanctuary. The end of it shall be with a
flood, and till the end of the war desolations are determined.
Then he shall confirm a covenant with many for one week;
But in the middle of the week He shall bring an end
to sacrifice and offering.
And on the wing of abominations shall be one who makes
desolate, even until consummation, which is determined,
is poured out on the desolate.
(Dan 9:24–27)

149

The first words of Daniel 9 indicate the historical context in which the prophetic word is uttered: "In the first year of Darius," that is from 538 to 537 B.C.E. This was a year loaded with events of hope. For Daniel, this year is marked by the miracle of the lion's den, the year of the visit of the angel of the Lord, who saves him from death (Dan 6). But it is also for him the year of the first fulfillment of his own prophecies (see Dan 2 and 7): Babylon falls into the hands of the new Medo-Persian kingdom. Lastly and above all, this is the year of the coming of Cyrus, who had been predicted by Isaiah as a messiah who would deliver Israel (Isa 44:28–45:4).

Daniel is now verifying the fulfillment of this prophecy with his own eyes. His present interest is all the more revived. He then consults the book of Jeremiah, where he discovers that the exile was to last 70 years (Dan 9:2). The starting point of the 70 years is 605 B.C.E., the very year of the defeat of Jerusalem (Dan 1). Now, 68 years have elapsed since that time. Yet nothing seems to suggest the end of the exile. The Jewish people still live in Babylonian captivity, and Jerusalem is still in ruins since 586 B.C.E. Daniel is worried. And out of anguish and hopelessness, he cries and prays to God. To Daniel's prayer, God's response takes the form of a messianic prophecy. It refers to the coming of the Messiah:

> Know therefore and understand, that from the going forth of the command to restore and build Jerusalem until Messiah the Prince, there shall be seven weeks and sixty two weeks. (Dan 9:25)

This is the only Biblical text that refers explicitly to the Messiah, and this is also the only biblical text that dares to situate that coming in time. Jewish historian Flavius Josephus seems to allude to this prophecy when he says about Daniel:

> He was one of the greatest of the prophets . . . for he did not only prophesy of future events, as did the other prophets, but he also determined the time of their accomplishment.[1]

This is therefore an extraordinary prophecy. Significantly this chapter begins with positive understanding (Dan 9:2) while the preceding chapter had just ended with negative understanding (Dan 8:27). The seventy-weeks prophecy is then placed in the perspective of a promise of understanding. Yet this text is not easy to understand as it confronts the reader with two serious problems. The first one has to do with the difficulty of the text itself, which is dense, written in poetry and full of rare words and expressions and whose syntax is particularly complex. The second that is somehow related to the first has to do with the multitude of interpretations which have been given to this prophecy by interpreters through the centuries.[2] These interpretations are generally divided on the issue of the historical application of this prophecy, depending on whether one believes in the historical fulfillment of this prophecy or not. Those who take its historical application seriously seek to find in the text clues to situate the time of the coming of the Messiah (Historical-Messianic interpretation, represented in traditional Jewish and Christian

---

1. Flavius Josephus, *Jewish Antiquities*, x, xi,.7; translated by William Whiston in *The Complete Works of Josephus* (Grand Rapids MI: Kregel Publications, 1960), 227.

2. For a summary of these interpretations, see James A. Montgomery, *A Critical and Exegetical Commentary on the Book of Daniel*, International Critical Commentary (Edinburgh: T. and T. Clark, 1950), 390–401; cf. Gerhard F. Hasel, "The Seventy Weeks of Daniel 9:24–27," *Ministry*, May 1976, 1D–21D.

sources and with some variations in Dispensationalism). Those who dismiss the historical significance of the text understand the prophecy as a *vaticinium ex eventu* referring to an event that already took place before the actual text, that is in the Maccabean period; they therefore identify the Messiah implied in this text as the priest Onias III (171–170 B.C.E.) who died during the persecution of Antiochus Epiphanes. The prophecy of Dan 9 mentions clearly a Messiah. The first and fundamental question to clarify concerns, then, the identity of this Messiah: Who is this Messiah? This prophecy surrounds this Messiah with particular events, and these events are situated within a chronological calendar with numbers and periods of time. The second question to address concerns, then, the historical moment of this Messiah: When will he come? What are the events that are related to him? To answer these questions, the Hebrew text will be our primary guide. The literary forms and poetic expressions will be closely observed, the rhythm of the discourse will be heard, and the words and expressions will be analyzed.

Poetic Analysis

When one considers this passage from a literary point of view,[3] one is struck by the fact that it moves like a seesaw between two poles, namely the people and their sins and Jerusalem with its sanctuary, thus responding directly to Daniel's prayer:

> O Lord, hear! O Lord, forgive! O Lord, listen and act!
> Do not delay for Your own sake, my God, for Your
> city and Your people are called by Your name (9:19).

---

3. This analysis follows closely my proposal in Jacques Doukhan, "The Seventy Weeks of Daniel 9: An Exegetical Study," *Andrews University Seminary Studies* 17, no. 1 (1979): 1–22.

This twofold nature of this prophecy is apparent in the prelude (v. 24), as well as in the body of the vision itself (vv. 25–27).

1. The Prelude (Daniel 9:24)

The two themes of the poem are first stated: "Concerning[4] your people [2 words] and concerning your holy city [3 words]." The next three poetic lines[5] come in the rhythm of 2 words each.[6] The thought is concerned with the sin and the forgiveness, ideas that Daniel related to the people (vv. 5, 7, 17). Then the following three poetic lines come in the rhythm of 3 words each. The thought here is cultic and cosmic, involving the specific notions of "righteousness" (*sdq*), "holy of holies" (*qodesh qodashim*), "vision" (*hazon*), which are associated with the theme of the holy city and hence with the sanctuary.[7] The poetic discourse of the prelude is then composed with two successive stanzas of different rhythm (2, 3) which have

---

4. We give here a literal translation; the Hebrew word *'al* means literally "on," "about," or "concerning" (see Jerusalem Bible), and not "for" as it has sometimes been translated (NKJV). Note that the same proposition *'al* is used a few verses earlier, with the same words: "for Your name is called on [*'al*] Your city and on [*'al*] Your people" (Dan 9:19 literal trans.).

5. Also called by the technical term *hemistich* (or *stich*).

6. Our poetic analysis takes into account the number of words rather than the number of accents, not only because this is the clearest and surest determination, but also because "the problem of the Hebrew metre is still unsolved" (Wilfred G. E. Watson, *Traditional Techniques in Classical Hebrew Verses*, Journal for the Study of the Old Testament: Supplement Series 170 [Sheffield: Sheffield Academic Press, 1994], 330).

7. For the association of *sdq* ("righteousness") with the sanctuary, see esp. Dan 8:14; Pss 4:6; 51:21; 132:9; Isa 61:3; for its association with the city of Jerusalem, see Isa 1:26; 33:5. For the association of "holy of holies" with the sanctuary, referring to holy objects belonging to the holy service of the sanctuary, see Exod 29:37; 30:29; Ezek 43:12; or to the whole Tabernacle or Temple, see Ezek 43:12; 45:3. As for the word *hazon* ("vision"), it points back to the same *hazon* as in Dan 8:13–14, where it appears in connection to the sanctuary.

been written face to face in the table below in order to bring in evidence the synthetic parallelism between them:[8]

A totality of 70 Weeks has been determined

Concerning your people [2 words]	Concerning your holy city [3words]
To finish the transgression [2 words]	To bring everlasting righteousness [3 words]
To seal [htm] sins [2 words]	To seal [htm] vision and prophets [3 words]
To atone [kpr] for iniquity [2 words]	To anoint holy of holies [3 words]

2. The Vision (Daniel 9:25–27)

In Daniel 9:25, the angel goes on: "Know therefore and understand." These two words (in Hebrew) stress the importance of the passage that follows, and they introduce the explanation. According to the same principle of parallelism, the message is developed in three phases.

The same twofold picture (people and Jerusalem) is present here. The vision contains God's answer to the prophet's anguished question about the fate of the people and the city of Jerusalem. In the extension of the theme "people" stands the figure of a Messiah as the response to the sins of the people; whereas in the line of the theme "Jerusalem" the historical destiny of the city and its sanctuary is revealed. This twofold structure is also confirmed from within, since each group (Messiah or Jerusalem) is characterized by the use of a common expression (in bold in the following table). Thus the three poetic lines concerned with the Messiah, regularly the first part of the verse (A[1], A[2], A[3]), have the word shavu'a (week) in common, situating in time

8. On the explanation of this parallelism, see Doukhan, "The Seventy Weeks of Daniel 9," 11.

154

events associated with the Messiah; whereas the three poetic lines concerned with Jerusalem, regularly the second part of the verse (B¹, B², B³), have the word *hrs* ("moat," "decree") in common, focusing on space, the desolation associated with Jerusalem with no situating in time:

From the going forth of the word to restore and build Jerusalem[9]

A¹ (v. 25a)
Coming of the Messiah
Until Messiah Prince [*nagid*], seven weeks [*shavu'a*] and sixty two weeks [*shavu'a*]

B¹ (v. 25b)
Reconstruction of the city
It shall be restored and built with squares and moat [*hrs*], but in troubled time.

A² (v. 26a)
Death of the Messiah
After the 62 weeks [*shavu'a*] Messiah shall be cut off without help

B² (v. 26b)
Destruction of the city
and the people of the coming prince [*nagid*], shall destroy the city, and the sanctuary. Its end will be in a flood, and until the end of a decree [*hrs*] there will be war; it will be desolation.

A³ (v. 27a)
Covenant of the Messiah
He shall confirm covenant with many for one week [*shavu'a*]; but in the middle of the week [*shavu'a*] He shall bring an end to sacrifice and offering.

B³ (v. 27b)
Desolation of the city
On the wing of abominations desolation until the end, which is determined [*hrs*] is poured on the desolating.

---

9. This phrase belongs to both thematic lines (A and B), since it is related to both future events, the reconstruction of Jerusalem marking the starting point of the period which leads to the coming of the Messiah. Also it does not contain any of the specific keywords (*shavu'a* or *hrs*), normally associated respectively to the two themes, the Messiah and Jerusalem. This phrase has therefore been put outside of the thematic lines as an autonomous feature on which depends the development of the two lines.

The two motifs of Messiah and Jerusalem are used alternately, giving this section its interwoven composition:

A^1	Messiah
B^1	Jerusalem
A^2	Messiah
B^2	Jerusalem
A^3	Messiah (here implied)[10]
B^3	Jerusalem

Indeed, the literary scaffolding of the prophetic text is marvelous. Yet this beauty serves a definite purpose. The prophet's message comes through the poetic dynamic of the text and the clues provided by its literary structure.

The Seventy Weeks

The first and basic question concerns the nature of these weeks. Are these "weeks" literal weeks of seven days or are they to be interpreted differently? A number of clues from within the immediate context of the prophecy, as well as from the book of Daniel at large, should help us determine the nature of these weeks.

---

10. This small paragraph must be related to the Messiah on account of the following observations: (1) the presence of the theme of the weeks, the key word related to the Messiah; (2) the principle of the interwoven composition (Messiah-Jerusalem-Messiah-Jerusalem-Messiah-Jerusalem); and (3) the notions of covenant and of cessation of the offerings that borrow the notions expressed in the verb *krt* ("cut off") of the preceding messianic paragraph (A^1). These last are one more token according to which A^2 lies on the same level as A^1 and follows it. Indeed, the word *krt* is an allusion both to a covenant (*krt* is the technical term which expresses the process of the covenant; cf. Exod 24:8; 34:27; Josh 9:15; Hos 2:20; Jer 34:13; etc.) and to a cessation. The word *krt* conveys already in A^1 the two theological meanings of the death of the Messiah, which we find again mentioned in A^2; namely, the covenant by his sacrifice, hence the end of sacrifices.

A Literary Play on 70

It is interesting that chap. 9 begins and ends with the number 70. The introduction of the chapter speaks about the prophetic vision of 70 years (Dan 9:2, cf. 2 Chr 36:21; Jer 25:11–12), while at the conclusion of the chapter Daniel speaks about 70 weeks (Dan 9:24). The fact that this same number is used in the beginning and the end of the chapter suggests an internal relation between the two measures. Indeed it has been noted[11] that if the first 70 is referring to the measure of sabbatical years, an interpretation that is well attested in the Scriptures (2 Chr 36:21; cf. Lev 36:34–35), the second 70 must accordingly refer to the Jubilee. While the first 70 is made of the multiplication of 7 years (sabbatical) by 10, the second 70 is made of the multiplication of 7x7 years (Jubilee) by 10. It is also interesting that the two prophetic periods lead to the coming of a messiah. The first 70 lead to the messiah Cyrus who saves Israel from the exile (Isa 45:1), and the second 70 leads to the universal Messiah who saves the world from sin.[12] The two prophetic measures echo each other, as an inclusio. Furthermore, in the Hebrew text the connection is confirmed in a literary manner; they form a chiastic structure.[13] The first

11. See P. Grelot, "Soixante-dix semaines d'années," *Biblica* 50 (1969): 169. Cf. Doukhan, "The Seventy Weeks of Daniel 9," 7.

12. This parallel between these two messiahs has also been noted in the book of Isaiah where the messiah Cyrus and the Suffering Servant are the two poles of liberation and atonement and echo each other in "a coherent and parallel development," see Kye Sang Ha, "Cultic Allusions in the Suffering Servant Poem (Isaiah 52:13–53:12)" (Ph.D. diss., Andrews University, 2009), 263; cf. J. Alec Motyer, *The Prophecy of Isaiah: An Introduction and Commentary* (Downers Grove, IL: InterVarsity Press, 1993), 353.

13. The same literary play is attested in the text of the call of Abraham in Gen 12:1–4, where the introduction and the conclusion echo each other through inclusio: "The Lord ... Abram ... Go (Gen 12:1) // Go ... Abram ... The Lord." (Gen 12:4).

phrase in Dan 9:2 is seventy years (AB); the second phrase in Daniel 9:24 is formulated backwards, weeks seventy (B¹A¹):

A 70   B Years (Heb. *shiv'im shanah*)

$$X$$

B¹ Weeks   A¹ 70 (Heb. *shavu'im shiv'im*)

The chiastic structure, which connects the two measures, hints at the nature of those weeks. By paralleling 70 with 70 and weeks with years Daniel gives us a clue of the nature of the weeks: they are weeks of years.

Weeks of Days Versus Weeks of Years

It is significant that in the next chapter (Dan 10:3) the biblical author uses the same particular form (*shavu'im*) for weeks,[14] as in chap. 9:24–27. This repetition of the same rare form (unique to these two passages in the whole Bible) suggests a special link between the two passages; yet the prophet feels necessary in chap. 10 to specify "weeks of days" (v. 2; literal translation). This is the only biblical text where this expression is used. The intent of this abnormal precision "of days" was, then, to distinguish these weeks of fasting from those he had just talked about a few verses before in chap. 9. The three weeks of fasting in Dan 10 are, of course, weeks "of days," while the 70 weeks of Dan 9 must be understood differently, as weeks of years.

---

14. These are the only two biblical passages where the word *îm* (weeks) is used in the masculine. Normally, the Hebrew plural for weeks has a feminine form (*ôth*).

The Day-Year Principle in the Bible

Outside of the book of Daniel, this equation "day equals year" is attested throughout the Hebrew Scriptures. Some forty years before Daniel another Exilic prophet, Ezekiel, who had also been exiled to Babylon, was given a vision which was also concerned with the destruction of Jerusalem in relation to the sin of his people (Ezek 4:4–7). For Ezekiel as for Daniel, the divine oracles concluded with the fixing of a definite time period. In Ezekiel's case, the time is decoded: "I have laid on you a day for each year" (Ezek 4:6). Considering the many parallels between the two situations, it is most likely that Daniel's 70 weeks (490 days) likewise meant years (490 years). But this usage does not just appear in specific isolated texts. In narrative texts, the word "days" (*yamim*) can often be used with the meaning of "years," and most Bible translations render the Hebrew word "days" with the word "years."[15] In poetic texts, many parallelisms relate the word "days" with the word "years": "I have considered the days of old, the years of ancient times" (Ps 77:5; Heb. v. 6); "To proclaim the acceptable year of the Lord, and the day of vengeance of our God" (Isa 61:2). This principle is also present in Levitical laws. It was implied in the institution of the sabbatical year and the Jubilee. Significantly, the seventieth year, or sabbatical year, was called a Sabbath just like the seventh day of the week (Lev 25:17). And the same language was used for the Jubilee (Lev 25:8).

---

15. See Exod 13:10; Judg 11:40; 1 Sam 2:19; 1 Kgs 11:42, etc.

The Function of the *Athnach*

Now, the fact that there is an *athnach*, the most important disjunctive accent, under the word "seven" in Dan 9:25 suggests that the seven weeks should be read separately from the following sixty-two weeks as suggested by the following translation:[16]

> From the going forth of the commandment to restore and to build Yerushalyim until an anointed prince, shall be weeks seven [*athnach*]:
>
> then for sixty-two weeks it shall be built again, with squares and moat . . .

According to this reading of the Hebrew text, which cuts after "seven weeks" because of the disjunctive function of the *athnach,* the Messiah should, then come after the first seven weeks.

But the use of the *athnach* does not always mean separation. It is often used to mark an emphasis.[17] Thus, in Gen 1:1, the *athnach* is put under the word *Elohim* (God) in the Hebrew phrase, *bereshit bara **Elohim*** ("in the beginning God created"),[18] obviously not to mark a separation between God's creative work and its complement object heavens and earth, but rather to emphasize the word ***Elohim*** the divine Author of creation. Should the *athnach* be taken as full disjunctive it would disturb the meaning of the sentence; it would read, "In

---

16. The Jerusalem Bible.

17. See William Wickes, *Two Treatises on the Accentuation of the Old Testament* (New York: Ktav Publishing House, 1970), part I: 32–35, part II: 4.

18. Literally, "in the beginning created God." In Hebrew syntax the verb comes before its subject.

the beginning God created. The heaven and the earth." Another example can be found in Gen 22:10 where the *athnach* is put on the word "knife": "And Abraham stretched out his hand and took **the knife** [*athnach*] to kill his son." Here also the *athnach* should not be interpreted as marking a separation; it expresses rather an emphasis on the knife, which threatens Isaac and thus suggests some kind of suspense.

Likewise in Dan 9:24, the *athnach* is put on the word "seven" to mark an emphasis because of the importance of the number seven in the prophetic message (see above our comments on the play on 70 appearing in the beginning of the chapter in the form of 7x10 and at the end of the chapter in the form of 7x7x10). The number 7 is also emphasized in the way the 70 weeks are divided. The theme of seven marks in 9:25 the beginning of the 70 weeks (7 weeks), and in 9:27, the end of the 70 weeks (1 week = 7 days),

Dan 9:25: shall be weeks **seven** [*athnach*] . . .

Dan 9:27: then he shall confirm a covenant with many for one **seven** [*athnach*].

Thus the *athnach* is used to emphasize the first and the last unit of seven of the prophecy, while in the middle we have the ordinary number of sixty-two:

7–62–**7**

The reason for this emphasis on the number 7 conveys the ideas of completion and final salvation, which are attached to the coming of this Messiah. Taking into consideration the emphatic function of the *athnach*, rather than its disjunctive function, the seven weeks should, then be read and understood in connection to the "sixty-two weeks," as suggested in the following literal translation:

> From the going forth of the word to restore and to build Jerusalem until Messiah prince,
>
> shall be **seven** and sixty-two weeks. (Dan 9:25)

The Starting Point

The coming of this Messiah is related to an earthly word (9:25), which concerns the reconstruction of Jerusalem. This earthly word (*davar*) marks the starting point of the prophetic period of the 70 weeks: "From the going forth of the command to restore and build Jerusalem" (Dan 9:25). Note that this "command" concerns directly the reconstruction of Jerusalem. As the Hebrew preposition *le* ("to") indicates, this word is an order "to restore and build Jerusalem." It cannot, therefore, refer to the word of Jeremiah, which is a prophecy about the return of the Israelites from Babylon (Jer 29:10; 25:12) rather than the actual command to rebuild Jerusalem.

The words "to restore and build Jerusalem" can, therefore, only apply to a future administrative decree,[19] which triggers the reconstruction of Jerusalem. The book of Ezra tells us that the city of Jerusalem was indeed "rebuilt and restored" following three decrees issued respectively by Persian kings Cyrus, Darius, and Artaxerxes (Ezra 6:14). The first decree, which was issued by Cyrus in 538 B.C.E., allowed the return of the first exiles. Within one year, some fifty thousand Jews

---

19. The usage of *davar* "word" for decree is attested in 2 Chr 30:5.

went back to their fatherland. But this decree essentially concerned the reconstruction of the temple. Ezra reports that five thousand four hundred articles of the temple were brought back from Babylon to Jerusalem (Ezra 1:11).

The second decree, which was issued in 519 B.C.E. by Darius I Hystaspes, or Darius the Great (not to be confused with Darius the Mede), only repeated and confirmed Cyrus' order.

The third decree was issued by Artaxerxes I Longimanus. A number of clues suggest that it is the decree which is to be considered in the prophetic computation:

1. This is the last decree and, therefore, the only one, which is effective. The very fact that we have three decrees indicates that the first two decrees were not carried out. It is also interesting to note that the word "command" or "decree" is used by Ezra in the singular to refer to the three documents together, thereby indicating the unity of the three utterances (Ezra 6:14).

2. This is the only decree to be complete, since it concerns the reconstruction of the temple as well as the restoration of the political and administrative structure of the city of Jerusalem (Ezra 7:25).

3. It is the only decree that is followed by a blessing to God:

   Blessed[20] be the Lord God of our fathers who has put such a thing as this in the king's heart, to beautify the house of the Lord, which is in Jerusalem, and

---

20. While in Ezra the Hebrew word for "blessed" is *baruk*, in Daniel the Hebrew word is *'ashrei*, which "appears as a synonym or a substitute for the term *baruk*" (W. J. Harrelson, "Blessings and Curses," in *The Interpreter's Dictionary of the Bible*, ed. G. A. Buttrick [Nashville, TN: Abingdon Press, 1962], 1:446; cf. S. Mowinckel, *The Psalms in Israel's Worship* [Nashville, TN: Abingdon Press, 1967], 47).

has extended mercy to me before the king and his counselors, and before all the king's mighty princes. So I was encouraged, as the hand of the Lord my God was upon me; and I gathered chief men of Israel to go up with me. (Ezra 7:27–28)

We should note, here, that this method of associating the fulfillment, the end of a prophetic period, with a blessing is attested within the book of Daniel itself:

Blessed is the one who waits and reaches the end of the 1335 days (Dan 12:12 NIV).

4. It is furthermore significant that from the decree of Artaxerxes on the text of Ezra shifts from the Aramaic language, the tongue of the exile, to the Hebrew language, the national tongue of Israel. It is the decree of Artaxerxes that has generated a linguistic transition, the very sign that the national restoration had begun.

5. Ezra's reaction to the decree of Artaxerxes reflects also his acute awareness of the significance of that decree. The echo between the verse reporting the king's consent to Ezra's request regarding the reconstruction of Jerusalem and the verse reporting Ezra's departure to Jerusalem is particularly eloquent in that respect: in both instances Ezra speaks about "the hand of the Lord upon him" (Ezra 7:6, 9, 28) and from then on the phrase becomes a refrain in the biblical chronicle of this story (Ezra 8:18, 22, 31; cf. Neh. 2:8, 18); the use of this particular expression at that very moment confirms again the prophetic significance of Artaxerxes' decree. Furthermore the reference to the

164

searching[21] of the Torah[22] in v.10, in causal connection to the preceding verses mentioning the day of his departure,[23] is another indication from the text that Ezra understood his journey as "a partial fulfillment of prophetic expectations":[24]

Ezra came to Jerusalem . . .

On the first day of the first month he began his journey . . . and came to Jerusalem according to the good hand of his God upon him.

For Ezra had prepared his heart to study the Law of the Lord.

According to the book of Ezra, Artaxerxes issued the decree some time in the seventh year of the king (Ezra 7:8), since this was the year when Ezra received the decree from the king and subsequently left Babylon to Jerusalem to implement the decree (Ezra 7:8–9, 11; 8:31). History informs us that Artaxerxes began to reign from the year 465 B.C.E, which is the year of his accession to the throne. Now, for the Bible, the first year of a reign is actually counted from the beginning of the following year (see Jer 25:1 and Dan 1:1, 2; cf. 2 Kgs 18:1, 9, 10).

---

21. The Hebrew word, which is used in this verse is *darash*, a technical word for "doing exegesis," "studying" and "seeking" the interpretation of the divine message (1Kgs 22:7; Eccl 1:13).

22. The alternative description of the Torah as not only "the law of God" (v. 14) but the "wisdom" (v. 25) suggests that Torah is to be understood in a broader sense than "law," see Derek Kidner, *Ezra and Nehemiah: An Introduction and Commentary,* Tyndale Old Testament Commentaries (Downers Grove, IL: Inter-Varsity Press, 1979), 63.

23. The verse is introduced by the causal conjunction *ki* ("for," "because").

24. K. Koch, "Ezra and the Origins of Judaism," *Journal of Semitic Studies* 19 (1974): 185–186.

Moreover, the years of the reign were counted in the Bible beginning with the autumn (month of Tishri), following the practice of the Persian system then in force. For the Mishnah as well as the Talmud, the year of reign in the Bible must begin in Tishri.[25] And since Artaxerxes took the throne in 465 B.C.E., it is necessary to place his first year of reign from the autumn of 464 B.C.E. to the autumn of 463 B.C.E. and his seventh year, therefore, from autumn 458 B.C.E. to autumn 457B.C.E.

The Messiah

The Events of the Messiah

According to the prophecy of the seventy weeks, three distinctive events associated with the Messiah should be expected to fulfill this prophetic period of weeks, namely: (1) the anointing of the Messiah (Dan 9:25); (2) the death of the Messiah (Dan 9:26); and (3) the universal covenant with the Messiah (Dan 9:27).

The Anointing of the Messiah

The first event that is predicted by the prophecy is situated exactly after sixty-nine weeks from the time of the decree and concerns the "anointed" (Messiah):

> From the going forth of the command to restore and build Jerusalem until Messiah ["anointed"] the Prince, there shall be seven weeks and sixty-two weeks. (Dan 9:25)

25. See *m. Rosh Hashanah* 1:1.

Since the decree "to restore and build Jerusalem" has been identified as Artaxerxes' decree, which took place on the year 457 B.C.E. we count 483 years (69 x 7), from the year 457 B.C.E. This computation leads to the year extending from Autumn 26 to Autumn 27 of our era.

The Death of the Messiah

The text of Daniel goes so far as to predict the death of the Messiah:

> And after the sixty-two weeks Messiah shall be cut
> off. (Dan 9:26).

The use of the verb "cut off" (*krt* in the Niphal form, a passive) suggests the violent character of the death of the Messiah. This verb is regularly used in the Bible to designate the execution of a criminal (Lev 20:17; Num 15:31), or, in a broader sense, a massacre (Isa 11:13; Mic 5:8).

According to the prophecy of Daniel, this violent death is supposed to take place after the sixty-two weeks (Dan 9: 26), which means somewhere in the course of the 70th week, that is during the time that covers the last 7 years of the prophetic period, hence from the year 27 C.E. to the year 34. The exact moment of this death is, however, indicated later in the text in connection to the end of the sacrificial system:

> In the middle of the week He shall bring an end to
> sacrifice and offering. (Dan 9:27)

The "He" who brings the end to the sacrifices belongs to the same phrase as the "He" who confirms the covenant and should therefore be the same person. It is also significant that the verb describing the end of "sacrifice and offering" is used in the same Imperfect form *yashbit* ("bring and end") as the verb describing the Messiah's death *ykkaret* ("cut off").

The one who brings an end to the sacrifices and the one who confirms the covenant is therefore the same person as the Messiah who is cut off. The three events belong together. The first lesson of this correlation concerns the time of the death of the Messiah. Since the death of the Messiah is connected to "bring to an end sacrifice and offering," it will, then, occur at the same time, that is in the middle[26] of the 70th week (3 days and a half), hence three years and a half after the year 27, which takes us exactly to the year 31 A.D.

The Universal Covenant

Another lesson from these correlations concerns the time and the meaning of the covenant, which will take place the last week (70th):

> Then he shall confirm a covenant with many for one week. (Dan 9:27)

It is important to understand that this covenant is directly related to the death of the Messiah. It is significant indeed that

---

26. When *hasi* ("midst") is in status constructus with a period of time (here weeks), it means always "midst" and not "half" (Exod 12:29; Josh 10:13; Judg 16:3; Jer 17:11; Ps 102:25; Ruth 3:8). The context of our passage does not yield the meaning of "half." It is concerned with a definite action (*yashbit* ["cause to cease"] in the imperfect). This is, according to the structure, related to ("cut off"), implying the idea of suddenness. The nature of this act (sudden destruction) points therefore to a specific moment in time (midst of the week) rather than to a duration of time (half of the week).

the verb *krt* ("cut off") that describes the violent death of the Messiah belongs also to the vocabulary of covenant. In fact the two words "covenant" (*berit*) and "cut off" (*krt*) are normally associated (Gen 15:18; Jer 34:13), for in Hebrew, we cut (*krt*) a covenant (*berit*).

In our passage, we find the same association: the Messiah who is "cut off" (*krt*) in v. 26, "shall confirm a covenant" (*berit*) in v. 27.[27] This interplay between the word *krt* describing the death of the Messiah in v. 26, and the word *berit* in v. 27, two words, which are normally used together, not only confirms that the one who makes the covenant and the one who dies is the same person (see above), the Messiah, but also suggests the Levitical significance of the death of the Messiah. Indeed through this language, the ritual of the Levitical covenant associated with the death of the sacrificed animal is implied (Gen 15:10; Jer 34:18). In other words, Daniel speaks about the death of the Messiah in terms that recall the sacrifice of the covenant in the Levitical system. The first words of the seventy-weeks prophecy already pointed in that direction. The purpose of the seventy weeks is to bring "atonement [*kpr*] for iniquity" (Dan 9:24). The Messiah is thus identified with the sacrifice of the covenant. His death should have an atoning effect, just like the sacrifice. The prophet Isaiah also used the same metaphor to describe the death of the Suffering Servant. The verb that introduces that covenant "shall confirm" implies however that the covenant was already in existence before; it is now "confirmed" (NKJV). The use of the verb *higbir* from the verb *gbr* ("strong") in the Hiphil (causative) form suggests a process that "causes to be strong," "strengthens" a covenant that

---

27. This association (*krt-berit*) confirms the reading that makes the Messiah (with *krt*) of v. 26 the implicit subject of the covenant (*berit*) in v. 27.

was already in existence. The covenant is made stronger, an idea confirmed by the object of this covenant, the "many" (*rabbim*), which connotes universality and implies a broader scope of the covenant extended to the nations (see Isa 53:11). This event is also marked in the prophetic calendar: "one week" (Dan 9:27). We should remember that the measure of "weeks" is always given to situate the moment of an event related to the Messiah:

> The anointment of the Messiah takes place at the end of the "seven weeks and sixty-two weeks" (Dan 9:24).
>
> The end of the Messiah takes place "after sixty-two weeks" (Dan 9:26).
>
> The bringing "an end to sacrifice and offering" takes place in the middle of the week (Dan 9:27).

It is therefore reasonable to think that here also the expression "one week" situates the moment of this strengthening-broadening of the covenant with the same Messiah. This event will cover the last week, the 70th, extending from the time of the anointment of the Messiah in 27 C.E. to the year 34 C.E.

The Identity of the Messiah

As we have already noticed, the history of Israel knows many particular messiahs. The priest Aaron (Exod 28:41; Lev 16:32), King Saul (2 Sam 1:14), David (1 Sam 16:6, 13) and even a foreign prince Cyrus (Isa 45:1) were called "messiah." But the seventy-weeks prophecy speaks of a different Messiah whose scope goes beyond the local and particular history of Israel, a Messiah with cosmic and supernatural dimensions.

Universal Messiah

Daniel was hoping for the return from the exile; and now, two years before the end, he hears about Cyrus, a messiah who will permit the exiles to return to Jerusalem. Daniel's prayer was concerned with the 70 years of exile which had been predicted by the prophet Jeremiah and whose end was viewed by the prophet as a sabbatical year (Jer 25:11; cf. 2 Chr 36:21). Yet a number of clues suggest that God's response in the seventy weeks prophecy moves beyond the local situation to the larger scope of the universal and the absolute.

1. A Jubilee Messiah versus a Sabbatical messiah. Indeed the 70 years (**7** x 10) predicted by Jeremiah involves a messiah associated with the sabbatical year (Cyrus), while the seventy-weeks (**7** x **7** x 10) involve a Messiah associated with the Jubilee. This special sabbatical year (also called the Sabbath of Sabbaths), coming after 49 (7 x 7) years, was understood as a time of "liberty throughout all the land to all its inhabitants," when humans and nature would finally return to their original free condition (Lev 25:817). This is why this Messiah is associated with the Jubilee, which symbolized the final redemption of Israel and eventually of the world in the very terms of prophet Isaiah:

    The Spirit of the Lord God is upon Me, because the Lord has anointed [*mashah*] Me [lit: "made me Messiah"] to preach good tidings to the poor; He has sent Me to heal the brokenhearted, to proclaim liberty to the captives, and the opening

of the prison to those who are bound; to proclaim
the acceptable year of the Lord and the day of
vengeance of our God; to comfort all who mourn.
(Isa 61:12)

2. Universalistic Language versus Particularistic Language.
   Furthermore, the words which are used in the prayer in a
   definite sense, referring to a local and particular condition
   ("our," "my," "of the people," "of God," etc.), as soon as
   they appear in the context of the 70 weeks, are suddenly
   used in an indefinite sense, expressing a universalistic
   point of view. For instance, the word "sins" (*ht*), which
   is used in 9:24–27 in an indefinite sense speaking about
   sins in general, is always used in 9:1–23 in a relative
   sense: "our sins" (v. 16), "sins of the people" (v. 20),
   "my sin" (v. 20), "we have sinned" (vv. 5, 8, 16). The
   same observation holds for the word "iniquity" (*'awon*),
   which is used in an indefinite sense in the context of the
   seventy-weeks prophecy (v. 24) and in a relative sense
   in the context of the prayer: "we committed iniquity" (v.
   5), "our iniquities" (v. 13), "the iniquities of our fathers"
   (v. 16). This is also the case for the words "justice,"
   "vision," "prophet," etc.

   We may now understand why the word "messiah" is
   also used in the context of the seventy-weeks prophecy
   in an indefinite sense, an exceptional case in the whole
   Hebrew Bible, since throughout the Hebrew Scriptures
   the word Messiah is always used with an article or in the
   construct state, thus referring to a particular messiah. This
   observation suggests that in the present context of the

seventy-weeks prophecy the word "messiah" should refer to the Messiah par excellence, the universal Messiah.

3. The ideal Davidic Messiah. It is also noteworthy that this Messiah is also called "prince" (*nagid,* v. 25),[28] a qualification, which appears mostly in connection with King David (2 Sam 5:12; 2 Sam 7:8; Isa 55:4; 1 Chr 11:2, etc.) or his descendants (1 Kgs 1:34–35; 1 Chr 23:22, etc.). The Messiah of the seventy weeks prophecy is therefore to be identified as the ideal eschatological Davidic Messiah of biblical and Jewish tradition, the Messiah who would bring the ultimate and universal redemption. This observation is confirmed by the fact that this Messiah has something to do with the *rabbim* ("many"; v. 27), a word, which has a strong universalistic connotation and is also associated with the Suffering Servant son of David (see our commentary on Isa 53:12).

---

28. Note that the Hebrew word *nagid* ("prince") is also used to qualify the prince who leads the destruction of the city in Dan 9:26b. The two *nagids* are different though and should not be confused with each other. The respective syntax of these two phrases clearly suggests two distinct and even contrasted figures. The first is *mashiah nagid* ("Messiah Prince") while the second is *nagid ha-ba'* ("the coming prince"). The first is associated with the construction of Jerusalem, the second is associated with the destruction of Jerusalem. The first is described as being killed, the second is described as aggressor, as indicated through the verbs *ba'* "come" (the verb *ba'* "come" is used in the book of Daniel to describe an aggressing army, see Dan 1:1 and most of its occurrences in chap. 11, esp. Dan 11:16 with the same form. Cf. the same usage in Ezek 1:4; 7:5; 20:29, etc.) and the verb *yashhit* "destroy" which is associated in Dan 8:24 with the oppressive power represented by the little horn. It is also significant that the term *nagid* is used in the book of Ezekiel to designate the leader of Tyre (Ezek 23:35), in a context that shares much common wording with our passage (this passage in Ezekiel is also the only other biblical reference with *nagid* containing an association with *mashah,* see Ezek 23:14). In this case this intertextual connection would suggest an allusion to some kind of cosmic conflict beyond the horizons of the historical Daniel.

Divine Presence

God's presence is, as usual in the Messianic texts, not explicit. Yet the biblical author provides enough clues to suggest that God is clearly implied in this prophecy. God is not just present implicitly by the simple fact that He is the One who sent this word (Dan 9:23). He is effectively present in the actual course of the prophecy itself. The syntax of the verbs and the specific nature of actions that orient the prophetic story testify to the divine presence. The intense use of the Niphal, also called "divine passive"[29] implies God as a subject before five verbs.[30] The first passive verb "determined" (*nektak*) is particularly important as it is syntactically related with six verbs through the *lamed* of purpose (to) introducing the infinitive:

> Seventy weeks are determined . . .
> To finish
> To make an end
> To make reconciliation
> To bring
> To seal up
> To anoint

This syntax suggests God's presence behind these seven actions. We should therefore read: "The 70 weeks have been determined [by God] . . . to finish the transgression . . . to anoint the most holy." God is the author of the redemption that is predicted in the seventy-weeks prophecy.

---

29. See Joachim Jeremias, *New Testament Theology: The Proclamation of Jesus* (New York: Scribner, 1971), 13.

30. See v. 24: "determined" (*nektak*); v. 25: "built" (*nivnetah*); v. 26: "cut off" (*yikareth*); v. 26: "determined" (*neheretseth*); v. 27: "determined" (*neheretseth*).

In fact, the actions themselves testify to their divine Subject. For only God can "finish the transgression," "make an end of sins," "make reconciliation (*kpr*) for iniquity," "bring in everlasting righteousness," "seal up vision and prophecy," and "anoint the Most Holy." The language is eschatological, universal and absolute, with the idea of definitive fulfillment and the perspective of eternity ("finish," "make an end," "everlasting," "seal up"). Also the nature of these actions presupposes God's exclusive involvement. Indeed God is the only one who "atones the iniquity." Significantly, the phrase "atone iniquity" (*kpr 'awon*) which is in the center of that preface (Dan 9:24) is only used in the Bible with God as a subject.[31]

It is also interesting that among the five Niphal forms, "divine passive," which implies God as a subject, the third Niphal, *yikkaret*, "cut off" (Dan 9:26), which is in the middle of the five, has the Messiah as its explicit subject. We have already noted that the Messiah should also be the subject of the verb that introduces the covenant in the phrase "confirm a covenant," since the word "covenant" (*berit*) is normally associated with the word "cut off" (*krt*) especially in the technical phrase *krt berit* ("make a covenant").[32] Being the subject of the covenant, the Messiah is identified with God Himself, since God is normally the One who makes the covenant; and the phrase *krt berit* appears generally in the Scriptures, especially in a theological context, with God as its subject.[33] It is also

---

31. See, for instance, Jer 18:23; Ps 78:38.

32. The association of *krt* and *berit* "appears frequently" (Gerhard F. Hasel, "*karat*," *Theological Dictionary of the Old Testament*, ed. G. J. Botterweck, Helmer Ringgren, and Heinz-Joseph Fabry [Grand Rapids, MI: Eerdmans, 1995], 7:349) in "the majority of cases:1–129" (Abraham Even-Shoshan, *A New Concordance of the Bible* [Jerusalem: Kiryat Sefer Publishing House, 1990], 563).

33. See Gen 9:9; 15:18; Exod 34:27; Deut 18:69; 2 Kgs 17:38; Jer 34:13;

significant that the only other passage in the context of Dan 9, where the word *berit* appears, is with God, the Lord, as its subject:

> I prayed to the Lord my God: "O Lord, great and awesome God, who keeps His covenant [*berit*]," (Dan 9:4)

The same reasoning holds in regard to the phrase "bring an end to sacrifice and offering" (Dan 9:27). The syntactical parallel between the verb "bring an end" (*yashbit*), and the verb *yikkaret* ("cut off"), both being used in the same Imperfect form, suggests that the two events belong to the same time and pertain to the same action. It has been concluded that the death of the Messiah and the end of the sacrifices belong together, and constitute the same event. The Messiah is therefore also the subject of the verb "bring an end," just as He is the subject of *yikkaret* ("cut off") and of *wehigbir berit* ("confirmed the covenant"). Yet only God can "bring an end to the sacrifice and offering," just as only God can "finish the transgressions" and "make an end of sins" (Dan 9:24). Indeed God's presence in the prophetic event merges with the Messiah's presence.

Daniel 9:24–27 in the Hebrew Bible

The Book of Daniel

The Messianic interpretation of the seventy-weeks prophecy is already supported from within the book of Daniel itself.

Ps:50:5; 2 Chr 21:7, etc.

The messianic intent of this prophecy is already suggested through the structure of the prophetic chapters (2, 7, 8, 10, 11, 12), which all climax with the same vision of the destruction of the earthly kingdoms and the messianic redemption of mankind.

Daniel 2 with the vision of the stone that struck the image and became a great mountain (2:35), meaning the establishment of the kingdom of God "which shall never be destroyed" (2:44, 45).

Daniel 7 with the vision of the Son of man coming from heaven entails the destruction of the earthly kingdom (7:11–12) and inaugurates the Kingdom of God "which shall not be destroyed" (7:14).

Daniel 8 with the vision of the heavenly "Prince of princes" (8:11, 25) ends with the destruction of the earthly evil power, "without human hand" and consequently leads to the kingdom of God (8:25; cf. 2:43).

Daniel 10 with the vision of Michael, "one of the chief princes" (10:13) ends with the final victory against the evil powers (10:21).

Daniel 11 with the vision of cosmic battles ends with the perspective of the "glorious holy mountain" and the destruction of the earthly evil power "and no one will help him" and hence in the hope of the kingdom of God (11:45).

Daniel 12 with the last vision of Michael "the great prince" standing up victorious against the evil powers (12:1), climaxes with the promises of the resurrection and the "inheritance" of the kingdom "at the end of the days" (12:13).

Lastly, the coming of the Messiah in Dan 9, like the coming of the stone in chap. 2, of the Son of Man in Dan 8, and of

Michael in Dan 12, marks an end (with the common word "end," 9:26; 8:17, 19; 12:6, 9, 13) in the same perspective of eternity (with the common word *'olam*, "everlasting"; 9:24; 7:14, 27; 2:44). From this pattern, it may be inferred that in the same manner chap. 9 should climax and conclude with a messianic vision concerning the redemption of mankind. The general prophetic thrust of the book of Daniel invites us to understand the seventy-weeks prophecy from a messianic perspective.

Daniel 8:24–25

It is also particularly telling that the same association of words is used to depict the conflict opposing the evil power and the Messiah in Dan 9:26 and the evil power and the Prince of princes in Dan 8:24–25: "destroy" (*yashit*), "people" (*'am*) and "holy" (*qadosh*).

Exodus 29:36–37

The language of Dan 9:24 echoes the text of Exod 29:36–37. These are the only two biblical passages, which use the same association of three specific words, namely, the atonement (*kpr*), the anointment (*mashach*), and the holy of holies (*qodesh qodashim*). This distinct echo suggests that, as the text of Exod 29:36–37 concerns the anointment of Aaron, the first high priest of Israel, the seventy-weeks prophecy is meant to relate the Messiah to the anointing of that first high priest in the history of Israel. Dan 9:24 identifies the Messiah as a new high priest (cf. Ps 110).

Isaiah 53

With Isa 53, Dan 9 shares especially the common idea of a redeemer whose suffering and death mean atonement for the

178

iniquity of the people. Both passages use the same association of three technical words for "iniquity" (*ht'* "sin," *'awon* "iniquity," *pesha'* "transgression;" Dan 9:24; Isa 53:4–5; cf. Isa 43:24; see above).

Both passages allude to the royal origin of this Messiah. In Isa 53, this allusion is given through the usage of the technical word "my servant" (*'abdi*), which is one of the most frequent titles for David (see above). In Dan 9 the same allusion is provided through the usage of the technical word *nagid* ("prince"), which is often used in the Bible to characterize the anointed Davidic king (2 Sam 5:2; 6:21; 7:8; 1 Kgs 1:35; 1 Kgs 14:7; 16:2, etc.)[34]; in the book of Isaiah the word *nagid* ("prince") designates specifically the ideal eschatological Davidic king (Isa 55:3–4), through whom an everlasting covenant will be made and nations will be reached (cf. Isa 52:15).

Lastly, the two passages describe in similar language the universal effect of the coming of the Messiah. The same expression *larabbim* ("to the many") with the same preposition *la* ("to the") is used. In Dan 9:27, the Messiah will confirm (Hiphil form) a covenant "with the many;" likewise in Isa 53:11, the Suffering Servant will bring justification (Hiphil form) to the many (*rabim*).

Psalm 22

With Ps 22, Dan 9 shares the common idea of the Messiah suffering and dying without any help for him. The connection between the two texts is indirect through the use of the obscure

---

34. Both words *'avdi* "servant" and *nagid* "prince" may even appear together in connection to David (see 2 Sam 7:8; 1 Chr 17:7).

expression *'eyn lo'* ("without for him") in 9:26, which appears to be the shorter form of *'eyn 'ozer lo'* ("without any help for him") in Dan 11:45.

If this is the case, we then have reason to believe that our passage alludes to Ps 22, which also uses the same expression *'eyn 'ozer* "without any help" (Ps 22:11; Heb. v. 12), referring to God:[35]

> May God, be not far [*rhq*] from Me, . . . for there is none to help [*'eyn 'ozer*]. (Ps 22:11; Heb. v. 12).

The allusion of Dan 9 to Ps 22 would, then, suggest that the death of this Messiah would be understood as an abandonment of God.

Summary

The exegetical analysis of the seventy-weeks prophecy in Daniel 9:24–27 provides us with the following specific information regarding the scope, the function, the time and identity of the Messiah:

1. Universal and divine character: the syntax of the text (indefinite/absolute versus definite/relative) and specific wording associated with **the** Messiah ("many") suggest that this Messiah has universalistic scope; it is **the** Messiah. And this Messiah manifests God's presence.

---

35. The verb *'zr* ("help") conveys the idea of protection and is most often used with God as the subject (see Gen 49:25; 1 Sam 7:12; 2 Chr 14:10; 18:31; Pss 79:9; 119:86), see E. Lipinski, "*'azar*," in *Theological Dictionary of the Old Testament*, ed. G. J. Botterweck, Helmer Ringgren, and Heinz-Joseph Fabry (Grand Rapids, MI: Eerdmans, 1995), 11:13.

2. Atoning and redeeming functions: the Levitical language of the text ("atone," "transgressions," "sins," "iniquity," "anoint," "most holy," "cut off," "covenant," "sacrifice and offering") and the specific scenario of the coming of this Messiah, namely, his anointment, his sacrificial death, and his covenant with the "many" suggest that the coming of this Messiah should involve definite spiritual consequences for humankind (end of transgressions and of sins, atonement for iniquity, and the bringing of everlasting righteousness), meaning the salvation of humankind.

3. Historical timing: the eschatological language of the text ("finish," "end," "everlasting," "seal up vision and prophecy," "from . . . to") suggests that the coming of this Messiah will fulfill a historical expectation. The times of his anointing, of his death, and of the broadening of his covenant are precisely indicated through the use of the unit of "weeks," which should be understood as "weeks of years." Starting from the "word" triggering the reconstruction and restoration of Jerusalem (Artaxerxes' decree, 457 B.C.E.), the seventy weeks lead to the anointing of the anointed after "69 weeks," in the year 27 C.E., to his death in the middle of the last week, in the year 31 C.E., and to the broadening of the covenant, during the last week of the seventy weeks, ending in the year 34 C.E.

Daniel 9:24–27 in Jewish Tradition

Qumran

The Messiah of Dan 9 is identified as the "messenger" of good news, peace, and salvation:[36]

> The messenger is the Anointed of the spirit, of whom Daniel spoke, "after the sixty-two weeks, an Anointed shall be cut off" (Dan 9:26). The "Messenger who brings news, who announces salvation" is the one of whom it is written, "to proclaim the year of the Lord's favor, the day of vengeance of our God; to comfort all who mourn" (Isa 61:2). (*11Q13*)[37]

Talmud

On the words "seventy weeks [of years] have been decreed [cut off]," the Talmud comments:

> This prophecy was given at the beginning of the seventy years of captivity in Babylon. From the restoration to the second destruction, there were 420 years, which makes a total of 490, or seventy weeks of years. (*Nazir* 32b)

Elsewhere the Talmud is more precise:

> A week in Daniel 9 means a week of years. (*Yoma* 54a)

---

36. For other evidences of messianic applications of the seventy-weeks prophecy in Dan 9, see Roger Beckwith, "Daniel 9 and the Date of Messiah's Coming in Essene, Hellenistic, Pharisaic, Zealot and Early Christian Computation," *Revue de Qumran* 10 (December 1981): 523–525.

37. Quoted in Michael Wise, Martin Abegg, Jr., and Edward Cook, *The Dead Sea Scrolls, A New Translation* (New York: HarperCollins Publishers, 1996), 457.

Midrash

The *Midrash Rabbah* follows this same line of interpretation. In explaining the verse "He shall make a strong covenant with many for one week" (Dan 9:27), it says:

> A week represents a period of seven years. (*Lamentations Rabbah 34*)

Since then, the Jews have remained faithful to this reading; and the most famous of the exegetes, such as Saadia, Raschi, and Ibn Ezra, adopted it unanimously. Likewise, Moshe Hadarshan interpreted the passage of Dan 9:26–27 as referring to the eschatological "king Messiah" who will bring salvation and everlasting justice:

> It is the King Messiah of whom it is written in Daniel 9:24, "to bring in everlasting righteousness." (*Bereshit Rabbati* on Genesis 14:18)

The messianic interpretation of this text is also defended by the great Jewish commentator Moses Nachmanides, who applies the seventy-weeks prophecy to the Messiah, "the Sanctified one of the sons of David."[38]

Parallel Texts of Daniel 9:24–27 Recognized as Messianic in Jewish Tradition

Daniel 2:34

> Dan 2:34 "You watched while a stone was cut out without hands." Reish Lakish said: "This is the King Messiah." (*Tanhuma Exodus 25:34*)

---

38. Quoted in Montgomery, *Daniel*, 398.

Daniel 2:35

This is the King Messiah who will come in the future to reign from the extremity of the world to the other extremity, as it is written in Daniel 2:35, "the stone that struck the image became a great mountain and filled the whole earth." (*Pirqei Rabbi Eliezer Pereq 3*)

Daniel 7:13–14; 2:35

As for the Messiah King . . . It is written in Daniel 7:13–14 "And behold One like the Son of Man, coming with the clouds of heavens and dominion and glory will be given to him." And in Daniel 2:35 "The stone that struck the image became a great mountain and filled the whole earth." (*Bamidbar Rabba, 13, 13.*)

He is the Messiah as it is written, "Behold One like the Son of Man, coming with the clouds of heavens." (*Tanhuma Genesis 27:30–32*)

The Son of man will come only when the generation will be either entirely righteous or entirely wicked . . . R. Joshua ben Levi raised this problem: "It is written in Daniel 7:13 'And behold One like the Son of Man, coming with the clouds of heaven,' but it is also written in Zechariah 9:9. 'Lowly and riding on a donkey.' [This means] if they are worthy, with the clouds of heavens; if they are not worthy, lowly and riding on a donkey?" . . . The king Sabor responded: "You say about the Messiah that He would come on a donkey . . ." (*Sanhedrin 98a*)

184

Daniel 9:24–27 in the New Testament

Luke 4:18–21

It is significant that Jesus inaugurated His messianic ministry with the liturgical reading of the text of Isaiah (Isa 61:1–3), which happens to foretell the coming of the Messiah in terms of a Jubilee:

> He went into the Synagogue on the Sabbath day, and stood up to read. And he was handed the book of the prophet Isaiah. And when he had opened the book, He found the place where it was written: "The Spirit of the Lord is upon me, because He has anointed Me to preach the gospel to the poor. He has sent Me to heal the brokenhearted, to preach deliverance to the captives and recovery of sight to the blind, to set at liberty those who are oppressed, to preach the acceptable year of the Lord." (**Luke 4:18–19**)

As Jesus refers to the principle of Jubilee, He situates Himself directly in the line of the prophecy of the 70 weeks, which describes the coming of the Messiah as a Jubilee time (7 x 7 x 10). And indeed Jesus presents Himself as the fulfillment of the biblical prophecy: "And He began to say to them, 'Today this Scripture is fulfilled in your hearing'" (Luke 4:21).

The preceding chapter tells us that the year, when this reading took place, was also the very year when Jesus of Nazareth submitted Himself to the *tevilah* (the baptism by immersion). On that occasion, according to the story of the Gospel, the heavens opened and the Spirit of the world above

came down on Him as a concrete sign of His "anointing" by
the Spirit (Luke 3:21–22).

This event is dated in the Gospel of Luke in the fifteenth year
of the reign of Tiberius Caesar (Luke 3:1, 23). Since Tiberius
began to reign on year 13 C.E.,[39] it follows that the baptism/
anointing of Jesus should have taken place during the Jewish
year from Autumn 26 C.E. to Autumn 27 C.E.[40] It happens that
this year is the very year that was predicted by the seventy-
weeks prophecy as the year of the anointment of the Messiah.

Matthew 27:46

The New Testament accounts on the death of Jesus do not
refer explicitly to the seventy-weeks prophecy of Dan 9, but
allude to it indirectly. The shout of Jesus on the cross "My
God, My God why have you forsaken me?" (**Matt 27:46**; cf.
Mark 15:34) which quotes Ps 22:2 (ET 22:1) in its Aramaic
rendering,[41] pointing to 'eyn 'ozer ("without any helper") of
v. 11 (Heb. v. 12), may well hint at Dan 9:26 'eyn ['ozer] lô
("without any [helper] for him").

When the Gospels tell us that when Jesus died he said: "It
is finished" (John 19:30), and at that moment, "the veil of the
temple was torn in two from top to bottom" (**Mark 15:38**; cf.
Matt 27:46), they may well allude to the Prophecy of Dan 9:27
that predicted the end of the sacrificial system (Luke 22:19,

39. We must remember that the monk Dionysus Exiguus (Dennis the Little)
erroneously fixed the beginning of the Christian era on January 1 of the year 754 of
the Roman era, which was four years after the birth of Christ.

40. See G. B. Caird, "Chronology of the New Testament," *Interpreter's
Dictionary of the Bible*, ed. Arthur Buttrick (New York: Abingdon Press, 1962),
1:601; on the reckoning system see Jacques Doukhan, *Drinking at the Sources*
(Pacific Press, 1981), 135, n. 186.

41. See the Targum version in *Miqraoth Gdoloth*, ad loc.

20; cf. **Heb 9:26[42]**). According to the testimony of the Gospels (Matt 27), this event occurred when Pontius Pilate was still in function as procurator (26–36 C.E.). Moreover, the Gospel of John records four Passovers between the anointment of Jesus (27 C.E.) and his death (John 2:13; 5:1; 6:4; 12:1), thus providing evidence that three and half years did indeed elapse during that time. This is the year 31 C.E. which happens to coincide with the year, which was precisely predicted by the seventy-weeks prophecy as the year when the Messiah would die of a violent death.

Acts 2:5

The book of Acts reports about the event of a universal covenant, when the message of the God of Israel exploded beyond the borders of Israel and reached out to the Gentiles. This process, which was initiated with the anointment of the Messiah in 27 C. E. and hinted at in his liturgical reading of the Jubilee text of Isa 61, is now for the first time beginning to be clearly manifested. The book of Acts tells about the coming of "devout men from every nation under heaven" (**Acts 2:5**):

> Parthians and Medes and Elamites, those dwelling in Mesopotamia, Judea and Cappadocia, Pontus and Asia, Phrygia and Pamphylia, Egypt and the parts of Libya adjoining Cyrene, visitors from Rome, both Jews and proselytes, Cretans and Arabs—we hear them speaking in our own tongues the wonderful works of God. (Acts 2:9–11)

---

42. For the allusion to Dan 9:27 in Heb 9:26 through common wording, see William L. Lane, *Hebrews 9–13*, Word Biblical Commentary, vol. 47 (Dallas, TX: Word Books Publisher, 1991), 229, n. nn.

It is interesting that this special event takes place just seven weeks after the Messiah's death, during the Feast of the Weeks, *Shavuot*, a feast, which points again to the Jubilee. Indeed just as *Shavuot* concludes the preceding 49 days (7 weeks), the Jubilee also concludes the 49 preceding years.[43] It is then significant that the Feast of the Weeks marks the last event that fulfills the Prophecy of the Weeks. Perfect timing also because, as Rabbi Irving Greenberg points out, "*Shavuot* evokes the hope of the universal covenant."[44] This is indeed the feast that commemorates the covenant between God and Israel when the people standing at Sinai responded by accepting the Torah, the contract that would bind them with the Lord.[45] Jewish tradition records that when God gave the Torah at Sinai, His voice resonated in "seventy languages, so that all the nations should understand" (*Exodus Rabbah* 5:9). Another tradition inferred the universality of that event from the very fact that it took place in the wilderness:

> Why was the Torah not given in the Land of Israel? In order that the nations of the world shall not say: "Because it was given in Israel's land, we do not accept it." Lest one group say: "In my territory, the Torah was given." Therefore the Torah was given in the desert, publicly and openly, in a place belonging to no one.[46]

---

43. On the relation between the Feast of the Weeks and the Jubilee, see J. Van Goudoever, *Biblical Calendars* (Leiden, 1961), 17.

44. *The Jewish Way, Living the Holidays* (New York: Simon & Schuster, 1993), 85.

45. This association is hinted at in 2 Chr 15:10–14; cf. Exod 19:1.

46. *Mekhilta de-Rabbi Ishmael* on Exodus 20:2.

According to the Book of Jubilees (6:17), a product from the second Temple period, *Shavuot* is celebrated as a symbol of the covenant that God made with humankind through Noah. It is also meaningful that the liturgical reading of the book of Ruth marks this feast; for through the reading of the book of Ruth the universality of the covenant is reminded. This is the story of a Moabite who joined the community of Israel and embraced their God: "your people shall be my people, and your God, my God" (Ruth 1:16).

But the most decisive moment for this universal covenant is recorded later in the book of Acts with the first appearance of Paul, alias Saul, (**Acts 7:58**) who, according to Acts 9, was called by the Lord "to bear My name before the Gentiles" (Acts 9:15), and for that purpose called himself "apostle to the Gentiles" (Rom 11:13). We are in the year 34 C. E. , when Stephen saw the heavenly vision of the "Son of Man standing at the right hand of God" (**Acts 7:56**); this was through a hint to Ps 110 an allusion to the new priestly function of the Messiah that was implied in the seventy-weeks prophecy in Dan 9:24 (see supra our comments to Exod 29:36–37).

The Messianic Time

Calculating the messianic time is suspect and dangerous. The Talmud records an ancient rabbinic curse uttered against those who engage in this enterprise:

> Rabbi Shmuel bar Nahman said in the name of Rabbi Yohanan: "May those who calculate the [messianic] end swell up, for they said: 'Since the designated time [calculated by them] came, and he [the Messiah] did not come, [they say:] he will no

longer come.' Rather, wait for him, as it is stated: 'Though it tarry, wait for him'" (Habbakuk 2:3).[47]

Does this warning apply to our case in our searching of the seventy-weeks prophecy? Certainly not, since it is clear from the context of this passage that the rabbis do not have the text of Dan 9 in mind but refer here to "the final redemption"[48] at the end of human history. Preceding immediately our curse, the text referred to Dan 7:25 and its prophetic period of "time, times and half a time" and spoke about the messianic end as a cosmic event which will "shake the heavens and the earth."[49] And immediately following the curse, a few lines further, they refer to Dan 12:12 "Happy is he who waits," to urge for patient waiting. If the rabbis implied the text of Dan 9 in their curse, they would have, then, referred to it.

The rabbis' point is not so much to prevent us from trying to "understand" the meaning of the seventy-weeks prophecy. On the contrary the book of Daniel insists on the importance of "understanding" the mysteries of prophecy; the word "understand" (*habin*) is a key word in the book of Daniel and is particularly prominent in the immediate context of that prophecy.[50] The rabbis' concern is about any human calculation which would determine the coming of the Messiah at the end of human history. Indeed the seventy-weeks prophecy deals primarily with an event that belongs to human history and is

47. *B. Sanhedrin* 97b, literal translation in *The Talmud, The Steinsaltz Edition,* commentary by Rabbi Adin Steinsaltz (Even Yisrael) (New York: Random House, 1999), 7:11.

48. See the Commentary in ibid. 10.

49. Ibid, 10.

50. See André LaCocque, "One of the most important contributions of the Book of Daniel is its novel insistence on the linking of faith to understanding" (*The Book of Daniel,* Eng. rev. ed. [Atlanta: John Knox Press, 1979], 191).

situated in time, while the final coming of the Messiah concerns a cosmic event that ends human history and therefore strictly belongs to the divine domain.

The rabbis' intention in this curse is rather to emphasize the principle that human elaboration should not prevail over the event itself. For only the event, more than any human reasoning, is the argument and should speak by itself. In other words, the rabbis recommend that we should not try to prove the time of the coming of the Messiah and establish it on the basis of our logic but rather wait for his coming; and only the event should be considered as the convincing proof. In fact this way of thinking is specific to Hebrew thinking which relates the word to the historical event and even identifies with it. The Hebrew word *davar* means both "word" and "history." The book of Chronicles is called in Hebrew *divrey ha-yyamim*, which may either mean the "words of the days" or "the events of the days." For in Hebrew the word and the event are identified. The Hebrew text of the seventy-weeks prophecy makes that connection. The same word *davar* ("word") is used to designate the prophetic word of the seventy-weeks prophecy and the concrete event that inserts it into the flesh of history:

> Understand the word [*davar*] understand the prophetic vision. (Dan 9:23).

> From the going out of the word [*davar*] for the purpose of restoring and building Jerusalem . . . (Dan 9:24)

This echo on the word *davar* emphasizes the point that the word of God is not just a sound to be heard or a spiritual truth to be meditated. The word is history. Not only the Hebrew term *davar* means both "word" and "event"; it also contains the idea that the word of God does not stay at the stage of the discourse but is designed to actualize as an event: it will be fulfilled. Twice before this text the prophet Daniel had already affirmed this historical substance of the "word." First in the introduction of the chapter, when he referred to the "word [*davar*] of the Lord through Jeremiah the prophet that He would accomplish" (Dan 9:2); second in the middle of the prayer, when he referred to God's "words" (*davar*), which He "has confirmed . . . by bringing upon us a great disaster" (Dan 9:12). In both occasions, the word of God meets historical reality.

Furthermore, the seventy-weeks prophecy does not just refer vaguely to history, applying abstractly as a theological principle to a number of different events.[51] The fact that it is associated with specific events, such as the return from the 70 years of Babylonian exile under Cyrus (Dan 9:2) and the decree for the restoration of Jerusalem by Artaxerxes (Dan 9:25) and even situated in time chronologically through the use of specific numbers (Dan 9:2–27)[52] indicates that only one particular event is here intended. The message of the seventy-weeks prophecy is not to be interpreted spiritually or symbolically as some interpreters have suggested.[53] The

51. See, for instance, the so-called "apotelesmatic" principle or "multiple fulfillment"; cf. Desmond Ford, *Daniel* (Nashville, TN: Southern Publishing Association, 1978), 49.

52. It is probably this observation that led Flavius Josephus to be amazed about Daniel's preeminence over other prophets "for he did not only prophecy of future events, as did the other prophets, but he also determined the time of their accomplishments" (*Antiquities*, x, xi, 7).

53. See Grelot, "Soixante-dix semaines d'années," 169; cf. Joyce G. Baldwin, *Daniel: An Introduction and Commentary*, Tyndale Old Testament Commentaries (Downers Grove, IL: Inter-Varsity Press, 1978), 176; John E. Goldingay, *Daniel*, Word Biblical Commentary (Dallas, TX: Word Books Publisher, 1989), 259–260.

intention of this text is to send its reader to history. The text is essentially concerned with a particular event that is supposed to take place in the real course of history.

On the other hand the theological dimensions of the prophecy, especially its strong spiritual, universalistic, and eschatological perspective[54] and the fact that the prophetic event is also associated with sacred numbers such as the numbers "seven" and "seventy" suggest a special direction for the interpretation of the prophetic event. Indeed the various applications to figures such as King Cyrus the Great or the prince Zerubbabel or the high priest Yehoshua ben Zadak or even Onias III,[55] do not fit the theological intention and the universalistic outlook of that prophecy, nor do they meet the times pointed by the prophecy.

Now, the fact that the events associated with Jesus of Nazareth, the time of his coming and of his death and of his messianic success beyond the borders of Israel, coincide with the very moments predicted by Daniel's prophetic word is particularly troubling. All the more troubling as one considers the highly spiritual and universal significance of these events.

Now, if the "word" has been confirmed by the "event," if history has met prophecy, it means that this Messiah is not just the Messiah of a scriptural tradition, not just the Messiah of a culture or a religious group among others; not just the Messiah of a theological idea. It means that this Messiah has

---

54. On the theological dimensions of the seventy-weeks prophecy, see Doukhan, "The Seventy Weeks of Daniel 9," 19–22.

55. On these potential candidates, see Louis F. Hartman and Alexander A. Di Lella, *The Book of Daniel*, The Anchor Bible (Garden City, NY: Doubleday & Company, Inc., 1978), 251–252; cf. Rabbi Hersh Goldwurm, *Daniel, A New Translation with a Commentary Anthologized from Talmudic, Midrashic and Rabbinic Sources* (Brooklyn, NY: Mesorah Publications, 1979), 262–264.

been proved from the argument of history: He happened. And therefore he is the Messiah for everyone, the universal Messiah who transcends cultures and religions. It is indeed significant that this historical fulfillment of prophecy has been used by the early Christians as the main argument to prove that Jesus was the true Messiah, rather than the theological or philosophical discourse.[56]

This approach follows the line of the Hebrew Scriptures where the revelation of God was not elaborated through the logic of the abstract demonstration. The God of Israel did not establish Himself through a theological or a philosophical argument or even through a mystical or an emotional experience. Instead God imposed Himself and surprised humans in the course of historical events. Only history should attest to God. Also, because He is the God who makes Himself known in history, He is the God for every one of us. History is the place that is shared by all of us, more than the culture or tradition that marks the specificity of our character and separates us from each other. Likewise, when the Bible speaks about the Messiah, that is the One who would fulfill all the hopes of Israel and humankind, it does not do it by appealing to our minds or our hearts to convince us or to touch us in order to force its truth upon us. Instead, the only biblical argument is the event to come.

---

56. The messianic interpretation is clearly attested in Christian exegesis as early as the second century, if not already in the time of Jesus, as suggested in some texts of the New Testament (see above). On the history of this interpretation, see Jerome in *Jerome's Commentary on Daniel*, trans. Gleason L. Archer, Jr. (Grand Rapids, MI: Baker Book House, 1958), 95–110; James Montgomery, *The Book of Daniel*, 47–49; A. Y. Collins in John J. Collins, *Daniel*, Hermeneia, ed. Frank Moore Cross (Minneapolis, MN: Fortress, 1993), 112–123.

Synthetic Table of Messianic Interpretation				
Key Text	**Biblical Parallels**	**Jewish Tradition**	**New Testament**	**Messianic Features**
Gen 3:15	Gen 4:25 2 Sam 7:12–13 Ps 110	Gen 3:15 LXX *Targum Pseudo-J.* on Gen 3:15	Gal 3:16 Rom 16:20 Heb 2:14 Rev 12:11	Seed Conflict Divinity Death Hopelessness Salvation
Num 24:17	Gen 3:15 Gen 49:9–12	DSS: CD 7:18–21 *Targum Jonathan* on Num 24:17 *Midrash Tanhuma* on Num 24:17	(Matt 2:2) (2 Pet 1:19) (Rev 2:28) (Rev 22:16) (Echoes bracketed)	Star Conflict Divinity King Salvation
Isa 7:13–14	Isa 9:5–6 Isa 11:1–2 Mic 5:2–3	Isa 7:13–14 LXX DSS: 1QH III *Baba Bathra* 75b *Sanhedrin* 98b *Sanhedrin* 99a	Matt 1:20–23 Matt 28:20	Sign Divinity Incarnation Salvation
Isa 52:13–53:12	Isa 43:24 Ps 22 Isa 7:13–14	DSS: 4Q491c 1QIsaa Sanhedrin 98b *Pesiqta Rabbati* pisqa 37 *Bereshit Rabbati* on Gen 24:67 *Tanhuma* on Gen 27:30 *Targum Jonathan* on Isa 52:13	Phil 2:9 Rom 15:21 Matt 8:17 Acts 8:32–35 1 Pet 2:21–22	Servant Divinity Hopelessness Humanity Sin Suffering Death Resurrection Peace Salvation Eternity
Dan 9	Dan 2, 7, 8, 11, 12 Dan 8:24–25 Exod 29:36–37 Isa 52:13–53:12 Ps 22	*Nazir* 32b *Yoma* 54a *Bereshit Rabbati* on Gen 14:18 Flavius Josephus *Antiquities* 18:63–64	Luke 3:21–22 Luke 4:18–21 Matt 27:46 Mark 15:38 John 19:30 Luke 22:19–20 Heb 9:26	Sevens Death Divinity Salvation Peace Eternity

THE LESSONS OF MESSIANIC PROPHECY

O ur exegetical study of suspected messianic prophecies has led us to the definite conclusion that these biblical texts are indeed "messianic prophecies." This conclusion has been established on the basis of the following observations:

First, our exegesis of these texts has revealed that they all indicate a clear messianic intention. These texts do not owe their messianic content to a rereading or to a reinterpretation of later traditions. They are messianic in their own rights.

Second, our intertextual reading of these messianic texts has demonstrated that the messianic identification of these texts has been confirmed by later parallel texts, within the Hebrew Bible, which have themselves, interpreted these texts as messianic.

Third, the five texts are related to each other, sharing common messianic features, either directly with each other or indirectly through their parallel texts, thus, not only confirming each other as messianic texts, but also upholding messianism as a biblical phenomenon.

Fourth, the five texts have also been recognized as messianic texts in Jewish traditional texts as well as in the New Testament, thus testifying from the outside to a popular tradition of messianic interpretation.

Now, if our conclusion is correct, if indeed these texts are to be considered as messianic, due to internal as well as external evidences, this should have significant bearing on the hermeneutic question, the way one looks at these texts and the way one understands and interprets them. But beyond these texts, the fact that their object lies outside of themselves in the historical fulfillment obliges us also to enquire for a historical verification. Furthermore, and perhaps more importantly and more dangerously this conclusion could have an impact on the Jewish-Christian discussion.

The Hermeneutic Lesson

The messianic interpretation of the Old Testament texts is often suspect and methodologically difficult to justify. It has been argued that in the New Testament writings as well as in Jewish traditional writings these texts were taken out of their original context in order to serve the apologetic purpose of proving the messianic identification. The messianic texts were, in fact, not meant to be messianic. What is missed, however, in this critical evaluation is the fact that the ancient Jews and early Jewish-Christians never claimed to have performed an exegesis of messianic texts. The messianic proof was never made on the basis of an exegetical argumentation. The reason, then, why these biblical passages were applied to the Messiah was not because they were exegetically proven to refer to the Messiah, or even because they were arbitrarily used as "proof texts," but rather because they had been preserved in the traditional memory as being messianic. A possible explanation for this trust in those texts is that it was traditionally believed that along with the Sacred Scriptures was transmitted an oral tradition of interpretation which already stemmed from the original setting of these texts, presumably originating from the biblical author himself.[1] Whatever the historical truth may be on that matter, the fact that messianic interpretations of the biblical texts are already found in the Hebrew canon and the fact that they are still attested in rabbinic texts—the Talmud and the Midrashim—while the Jewish-Christian controversy was still going full blast, constitutes an important evidence of their authenticity and profound rooting in the Jewish consciousness (this also by the same token attests to the honesty of the scribes who transmitted these traditions).

It is also noteworthy that in the process of the discussion the Jew or the Jewish-Christian did not need to perform a thorough exegesis of the messianic text. A mere reference was enough. The question whether these texts were indeed originally intended to be messianic is a modern question and was irrelevant then. Only later, when the testimony of the traditional messianic interpretations of these biblical texts

---

1. The proof text for this view is traditionally taken from Deut 31:19, where Moses was asked to "teach" the Torah to the children of Israel and "put it in their mouths," that is, orally. For the Talmudic support of that tradition; see *Shab.*,31a (cf. also *Sif Num.*, 134; cf. Mark 23:2 ff.).

was no longer taken at face value, did it become necessary to submit them to the exegetical trial.

Now if the exegetical scrutiny of the texts leads to the conclusion that these texts were indeed meant to be messianic, it follows that the actual messianic interpretations as attested in the New Testament and even in Jewish tradition were not at odds with the original intention of the texts. The Jews who identified Jesus of Nazareth as their Messiah were then exegetically correct to do so. And if they were exegetically correct, it implies tremendous implications in regard to the hermeneutical questions.

First of all, it suggests a lesson concerning the interpretation of these texts. If indeed these texts were meant to be messianic, intentionally pointing only to a future Messiah, beyond their time, this obliges us to a significant nuance in our interpretation of these texts. Without questioning the validity of other cases, where rereading and typology may be the adequate interpretations, these texts testify also to the possibility for originally intended messianic prophecies. For these particular cases there is no room, then, neither to the "single meaning" interpretation which excludes any reference to the future or to all the other interpretations which tolerate the reference to the future along with the reference to the contemporary situation ("dual meaning," "re-lecture," typological"). The unique purpose of these messianic texts is messianic, and although they are articulated within a contemporary situation, and bring a word of comfort, which also responds to the contemporary concern, the message they carry is essentially future and is not the product of the contemporary imagination.

Second, it obliges us to recognize that these texts have indeed a predictive quality. The Bible is not just a piece of literature with high spiritual messages merely reflecting a contemporary situation. Its words transcend the cultural and historical setting and witness to a supernatural origin with a universal intention. The God who spoke in the past of biblical Israel remains, therefore, still relevant beyond that ancient time when the words were then written. This awareness means also a lesson that concerns the nature of the reading of those texts, suggesting that Faith, that is the belief in the divine Presence, is not foreign to the exegetical enterprise.

Lastly, it suggests a lesson concerning the connection between the so-called Old Testament and New Testament. If the New Testament writings testify to an event, which was predicted in the Old Testament, this means that the Old Testament and the New Testament belong together and are the product of the same inspiration. Indeed, they are not speaking independently, as if they were testifying to two heterogeneous truths, which would project themselves either in divergent or even in parallel directions and never meet. Instead, the Old Testament and the New Testament move toward each other and are meant to confirm, complement, and enrich each other. Messianic prophecies hint not only at the inspiration of the Scriptures but also their unity.

The Historical Lesson

And yet, history seems to contradict the Christian "messianic" interpretation of the biblical texts. If the Messiah has already come why are we still here? Why has history

201

continued its course, with no change whatsoever, as if nothing happened? Why do we need a second coming of the Messiah to meet this requirement? These questions are legitimate and most reasonable. Yet they overlook a very important historical fact. If the coming of the Messiah Jesus had brought with it the end of human history, this would have meant that He had come only for the Palestinian Jews of the first century, without even the awareness of all the other Jews and human beings of the world. In other words, the first coming of the Messiah in the tormented flesh of history was necessary, precisely in order to give to the messianic event its universal scope and character. Paradoxically, this need for a universal application of the messianic event that is sometimes used as an argument *against* the messianic claim of Jesus may well, in fact, be used as an argument *for* His messiahship. It is, indeed, remarkable that only the coming of Jesus has brought the light of Israel with this message of hope, and love, and peace beyond the local borders of time and space. This observation has been verified from the point of view of Jewish-Christian history; for without the Christian testimony, the message of Israel would have remained secluded within the narrow limits of its space and might have disappeared from the scene of history.[2]

But most of all, this observation has been powerfully confirmed in messianic history. It is, indeed, significant that after Jesus a great number of Messiahs rose in Israel's history. From the warrior Simeon Bar-Kokhba of Palestine in the second century, to the mystic Shabbetai Tsevi of Smyrna in the seventeenth century, and even nowadays to Rabbi Menahem Mendel Schneerson of New York, there has been a

2. See Doukhan, *Israel and the Church*, 94–95.

continuous chain of messianic pretenders.[3] All these messiahs drew crowds to themselves. Yet history does not retain them as messiahs anymore. Each movement was a short-lived flame, which did not extend its fire beyond the space and time of those messiahs. History provides the test for the true Messiah. This criteria for true messianism is affirmed in Judaism. Speaking of all the messianic movements which appear and disappear in the course of Jewish history, Berger acknowledges "The reason that such movements do not last goes to one of the most fundamental messianic convictions in Judaism: failure is failure."[4] We can recall here the point made by the Pharisee Raban Gamaliel, disciple of the great Hillel, when confronted with the question whether Jesus qualified as the true Messiah: "If this plan or this work is of men, it will come to nothing; but if it is of God, you cannot overthrow it" (Acts 5:38–39). Gamaliel was then referring to an old rabbinical principle attested later in a proverb pronounced by the Palestinian Tana of the second century, Johanan ha-sandlar: "Any community that is inspired from heaven will establish itself but what is not inspired from heaven will not."[5]

It is amazing, indeed, that Jesus, the first and hence the most ancient Jewish Messiah, also happens to be the only one that we still talk about, the only one who still has disciples, the only one who has been carried beyond the frontiers of space and time, the only one that has been systematically related to the messianic prophecies of the Hebrew Scriptures. This is an interesting and troubling fact that merits consideration.

---

3. For a listing of these messiahs, see Dan Cohn-Sherbok, *The Jewish Messiah* (Edinburgh: T & T Clark, 1997), 193–194.

4. Berger, 21.

5. *Pirke Aboth*, IV:14.

The Jewish-Christian Lesson

Yet the problem remains. After two-thousand years of painful history, the Christians have not been able to prove to the Jews that Jesus was the Messiah. And at the end of our demonstration, we must pause and honestly recognize that the messianic argument is not enough to trigger conviction. Even if we believe that the messianic texts are providing us with the proof that Jesus was indeed the Messiah, they still remain secondary in the decision. The reaction I usually receive when I present this material to Christians and to Jews is a perfect illustration of this observation.

When I present this material and all these arguments to Christians, they are often amazed and excited; and they always respond in the same manner with the same question: "How come then, that with all these proofs, the Jews have still not recognized Jesus as the Messiah?" My answer to the Christians' question is then: "Did you know all these proofs before?" And they always recognize that they did not. "How come then," I reply, "that you were able to recognize Jesus as the Messiah without all these proofs?"

When I present the same material and the same messianic prophecies to Jews, they are intrigued or angry, and always confront me with the same question: "If your proofs are so convincing, how is it that we never heard anything like this from our rabbis?" The very fact that this testimony was not given by the rabbis raises suspicion, all the more as this interpretation has traditionally been carried by Christians.

Both reactions, the Jewish and the Christian, show that proofs based solely on rational argumentation are not enough to bring about conviction. However powerful the argument may be, it still remains within the domain of abstraction. More convincing than the words and dialectics is the real experience in life. Remarkably, the Gospel record does not give even one case of "conversion" based exclusively on rational or even Scriptural demonstration. In fact, when "conversion" happened, it came from a different direction. Acceptance derived from the experience of a personal encounter with a person, the Messiah Himself, or when He was no longer there, with someone who experienced that encounter and testified to it. And from there, they would move to the next step and "understand" the Scriptures. A study of the Scriptures brings a ratification, an illumination of the choice rather than a demonstration of it. And even then, the living influence of the Other is needed.

Luke's story about our two Emmaus friends is an eloquent and powerful illustration to that process. Ironically, the two friends had already heard about these messianic prophecies, they had already studied them, and yet on their way to Emmaus, they were still doubting and unable to believe, as it is implied in Jesus' rebuke:

> O foolish ones, and slow of heart to believe in all
> that the prophets have spoken! Ought not the Christ
> to have suffered these things and to enter into His
> glory? (Luke 24:25–26).

Even "when Jesus himself drew near and went with them" (Luke 24:15), they still did not understand: "Their eyes were restrained and they did not know him" (Luke 24:16). And they were still debating (Luke 24:17).

205

Even when Jesus Himself taught to them, from the basics, "beginning at Moses and all the prophets, He expounded to them in all the Scriptures the things concerning Himself" (Luke 24:27). Even then the text reports no reaction on their part. They simply contend themselves to be hospitable and invite him to stay with them because the night was coming (Luke 24:29).

It is only later when "He sat at the table with them, that He took bread, blessed and broke it, and gave it to them. Then their eyes were opened and they knew Him" (Luke 24:30-31). Only after they met Him personally and recognized His familiar moves, then, suddenly the Scriptures became clear to them.[6] Significantly, this is the chronological sequence they retain as they reminisce about the last events. The "opening" of the Scriptures, follows and responds to the "opening" of their eyes about who He was:

> Did not our heart burn within us while He talked with
> us on the road, and while He opened the Scriptures
> to us? (Luke 24:32)

Certainly, this lesson applies to our study of the messianic prophecies. Even if the messianic prophecies were indeed intended to refer to this Messiah, even if the demonstration conducted in these pages was convincing, the doubt will

---

6. The validity of this principle is reaffirmed later when the Emmaus disciples join the other disciples in Jerusalem. In the beginning they are troubled and do not believe (Luke 24:37–39), although they had already studied the messianic prophecies (Luke 24:44); it is only when they meet and recognize Jesus, only when He eats with them that His explanation of the messianic prophecies makes sense to them. And even then they do not understand these texts by themselves; they still need Him to open "their understanding, that they might comprehend the Scriptures" (Luke 24:45).

always remain because the argument is not enough. As long as the Messiah is not really here in a personal encounter with Him, as long as we do not recognize His familiar moves, Martin Buber's question which started our walk into the texts of messianic prophecy will stand before us: "Were You here before?" A necessary question to force again and again our search into these texts. And who knows? The Messiah may surprise us on the way to Emmaus.

ABOUT THE AUTHOR

Dr. Jacques Benyamin Doukhan, who was educated in France, Israel, and the United States, holds a doctorate in Hebrew and Jewish Studies (D.Heb.Lett.) from the University of Strasbourg and a second doctorate in Theology (Th.D.) from Andrews University. He was also the recipient of a post-doctorate research scholarship from the Hebrew University of Jerusalem and holds a Master in Egyptology from the University of Montpellier. The eldest son of a religious Jewish family (Sephardic) and a former Yeshiva student, Doukhan has been confronted with the message of the Gospel along with the values and truths of his Jewish heritage and has hence challenged the Jewish-Christian tension. He is currently professor of Hebrew Language, Exegesis, and Jewish Studies, and director of the Institute of Jewish-Christian Studies at Andrews University. For many years he was the editor of *Shabbat Shalom* and *L'Olivier*, two journals devoted to Jewish-Christian rapprochement. He has authored many books including *Hebrew for Theologians: A Textbook for the Study of Biblical Hebrew in Relation to Hebrew Thinking*; *Secrets of Daniel: Wisdom and Dreams of a Jewish Prince in Exile*; *Israel and the Church: Two Voices for the Same God*; forthcoming *The Face of My Brother: Israel, Islam, and the Church*; and edited *Thinking in the Shadow of Hell: The Impact of the Holocaust on Theology and Jewish-Christian Relations*.

209

OTHER RELATED RESOURCES

Complete Jewish Bible: *A New English Version*
—Dr. David H. Stern

Presenting the Word of God as a unified Jewish book, the *Complete Jewish Bible* is a new version for Jews and non-Jews alike. It connects Jews with the Jewishness of the Messiah, and non-Jews with their Jewish roots. Names and key terms are returned to their original Hebrew and presented in easy-to-understand transliterations, enabling the reader to say them the way Yeshua (Jesus) did! 1697 pages.

Hardback	978-9653590151	**JB12**	$34.99
Paperback	978-9653590182	**JB13**	$29.99
Leather Cover	978-9653590199	**JB15**	$59.99
Large Print (12 Pt font)	978-1880226483	**JB16**	$49.99

Also available in French and Portuguese.

Jewish New Testament
—Dr. David H. Stern

The New Testament is a Jewish book, written by Jews, initially for Jews. Its central figure was a Jew. His followers were all Jews; yet no other version really communicates its original, essential Jewishness. Uses neutral terms and Hebrew names. Highlights Jewish references and corrects mistranslations. Freshly translated into English from Greek, this is a must read to learn about first-century faith. 436 pages

Hardback	978-9653590069	**JB02**	$19.99
Paperback	978-9653590038	**JB01**	$14.99
Spanish	978-1936716272	**JB17**	$24.99

Also available in French, German, Polish, Portuguese and Russian.

Jewish New Testament Commentary
—Dr. David H. Stern

This companion to the *Jewish New Testament* enhances Bible study. Passages and expressions are explained in their original cultural context. 15 years of research. 960 pages.

Hardback	978-9653590083	**JB06**	$34.99
Paperback	978-9653590113	**JB10**	$29.99

Psalms & Proverbs Tehillim תְּהִלִּים-*Mishlei* מִשְׁלֵי
—Translated by Dr. David Stern

Contemplate the power in these words anytime, anywhere: Psalms-*Tehillim* offers uplifting words of praise and gratitude, keeping us focused with the right attitude; Proverbs-*Mishlei* gives us the wisdom for daily living, renewing our minds by leading us to examine our actions, to discern good from evil, and to decide freely to do the good. Makes a wonderful and meaningful gift. Softcover, 224 pages.

978-1936716692	LB90	$9.99

Messianic Judaism *A Modern Movement With an Ancient Past*
—David H. Stern

An updated discussion of the history, ideology, theology and program for Messianic Judaism. A challenge to both Jews and non-Jews who honor Yeshua to catch the vision of Messianic Judaism. 312 pages

| | 978-1880226339 | **LB62** | $17.99 |

Restoring the Jewishness of the Gospel
A Message for Christians
—David H. Stern

Introduces Christians to the Jewish roots of their faith, challenges some conventional ideas, and raises some neglected questions: How are both the Jews and "the Church" God's people? Is the Law of Moses in force today? Filled with insight! Endorsed by Dr. Darrell L. Bock. 110 pages

| English | 978-1880226667 | **LB70** | $9.99 |
| Spanish | 978-9653590175 | **JB14** | $9.99 |

Come and Worship *Ways to Worship from the Hebrew Scriptures*
—Compiled by Barbara D. Malda

We were created to worship. God has graciously given us many ways to express our praise to him. Each way fits a different situation or moment in life, yet all are intended to bring honor and glory to him. When we believe that he is who he says he is [see *His Names are Wonderful!*] and that his Word is true, worship flows naturally from our hearts to his. Softcover, 128 pages.

| | 978-1936716678 | **LB88** | $9.99 |

His Names Are Wonderful
Getting to Know God Through His Hebrew Names
—Elizabeth L. Vander Meulen and Barbara D. Malda

In Hebrew thought, names did more than identify people; they revealed their nature. God's identity is expressed not in one name, but in many. This book will help readers know God better as they uncover the truths in his Hebrew names. 160 pages.

| | 978-1880226308 | **LB58** | $9.99 |

The Return of the Kosher Pig *The Divine Messiah in Jewish Thought*
—Rabbi Tzahi Shapira

The subject of Messiah fills many pages of rabbinic writings. Hidden in those pages is a little known concept that the Messiah has the same authority given to God. Based on the Scriptures and traditional rabbinic writings, this book shows the deity of Yeshua from a new perspective. You will see that the rabbis of old expected the Messiah to be divine. Softcover, 352 pages.

"One of the most interesting and learned tomes I have ever read. Contained within its pages is much with which I agree, some with which I disagree, and much about which I never thought. Rabbi Shapria's remarkable book cannot be ignored."

—Dr. Paige Patterson, President, Southwest Baptist Theological Seminary

| | 978-1936716456 | **LB81** | $ 39.99 |

Matthew Presents Yeshua, King Messiah *A Messianic Commentary*
—Rabbi Barney Kasdan

Few commentators are able to truly present Yeshua in his Jewish context. Most don't understand his background, his family, even his religion, and consequently really don't understand who he truly is. This commentator is well versed with first-century Jewish practices and thought, as well as the historical and cultural setting of the day, and the 'traditions of the Elders' that Yeshua so often spoke about. Get to know Yeshua, the King, through the writing of another rabbi, Barney Kasdan. 448 pages

978-1936716265   **LB76** $29.99

James the Just Presents Application of Torah
A Messianic Commentary
—Dr. David Friedman

James (Jacob) one of the Epistles written to first century Jewish followers of Yeshua. Dr. David Friedman, a former Professor of the Israel Bible Institute has shed new light for Christians from this very important letter.

978-1936716449   **LB82** $14.99

Jude On Faith and the Destructive Influence of Heresy
A Messianic Commentary
—Rabbi Joshua Brumbach

Almost no other canonical book has been as neglected and overlooked as the Epistle of Jude. This little book may be small, but it has a big message that is even more relevant today as when it was originally written.

978-1-936716-78-4   **LB97** $14.99

Conveying Our Heritage A Messianic Jewish Guide to Home Practice
—Daniel C. Juster, Th.D. Patricia A. Juster

Throughout history the heritage of faith has been conveyed within the family and the congregation. The first institution in the Bible is the family and only the family can raise children with an adequate appreciation of our faith and heritage. This guide exists to help families learn how to pass on the heritage of spiritual Messianic Jewish life. Softcover, 86 pages

978-1936716739   **LB93** $8.99

Mutual Blessing *Discovering the Ultimate Destiny of Creation*
—Daniel C. Juster

To truly love as God loves is to see the wonder and richness of the distinct differences in all of creation and his natural order of interdependence. This is the way to mutual blessing and the discovery of the ultimate destiny of creation. Learn how to become enriched and blessed as you enrich and bless others and all that is around you! Softcover, 135 pages.

978-1936716746   **LB94** $9.99

At the Feet of Rabbi Gamaliel
Rabbinic Influence in Paul's Teachings
—David Friedman, Ph.D.

Paul (Shaul) was on the "fast track" to becoming a sage and Sanhedrin judge, describing himself as passionate for the Torah and the traditions of the fathers, typical for an aspiring Pharisee: "...trained at the feet of Gamaliel in every detail of the Torah of our forefathers. I was a zealot for God, as all of you are today" (Acts 22.3, CJB). Did Shaul's teachings reflect Rabbi Gamaliel's instructions? Did Paul continue to value the Torah and Pharisaic tradition? Did Paul create a 'New' Theology? The results of the research within these pages and its conclusion may surprise you. Softcover, 100 pages.

978-1936716753 **LB95** $8.99

Debranding God *Revealing His True Essence*
—Eduardo Stein

The process of 'debranding' God is to remove all the labels and fads that prompt us to understand him as a supplier and ourselves as the most demanding of customers. Changing our perception of God also changes our perception of ourselves. In knowing who we are in relationship to God, we discover his, and our, true essence. Softcover, 252 pages.

978-1936716708 **LB91** $16.99

Under the Fig Tree *Messianic Thought Through the Hebrew Calendar*
—Patrick Gabriel Lumbroso

Take a daily devotional journey into the Word of God through the Hebrew Calendar and the Biblical Feasts. Learn deeper meaning of the Scriptures through Hebraic thought. Beautifully written and a source for inspiration to draw closer to Adonai every day. Softcover, 407 pages.

978-1936716760 **LB96** $25.99

Under the Vine *Messianic Thought Through the Hebrew Calendar*
—Patrick Gabriel Lumbroso

Journey daily through the Hebrew Calendar and Biblical Feasts into the B'rit Hadashah (New Testament) Scriptures as they are put in their rightful context, bringing Judaism alive in it's full beauty. Messianic faith was the motor and what gave substance to Abraham's new beliefs, hope to Job, trust to Isaac, vision to Jacob, resilience to Joseph, courage to David, wisdom to Solomon, knowledge to Daniel, and divine Messianic authority to Yeshua. Softcover, 412 pages.

978-1936716654 **LB87** $25.99

The Revolt of Rabbi Morris Cohen
Exploring the Passion & Piety of a Modern-day Pharisee
—Anthony Cardinale

A brilliant school psychologist, Rabbi Morris Cohen went on a one-man strike to protest the systematic mislabeling of slow learning pupils as "Learning Disabled" (to extract special education money from the state). His disciplinary hearing, based on the transcript, is a hilarious read! This effusive, garrulous man with an irresistible sense of humor lost his job, but achieved a major historic victory causing the reform of the billion-dollar special education program. Enter into the mind of an eighth-generation Orthodox rabbi to see how he deals spiritually with the loss of everything, even the love of his children. This modern-day Pharisee discovered a trusted friend in the author (a born again believer in Jesus) with whom he could openly struggle over Rabbinic Judaism as well as the concept of Jesus (Yeshua) as Messiah. Softcover, 320 pages.

978-1936716722   **LB92** $19.99

Stories of Yeshua
—Jim Reimann, Illustrator Julia Filipone-Erez

Children's Bible Storybook with four stories about Yeshua (Jesus).
Yeshua is Born: The Bethlehem Story based on Lk 1:26-35 & 2:1-20; *Yeshua and Nicodemus in Jerusalem* based on Jn 3:1-16; *Yeshua Loves the Little Children of the World* based on Matthew 18:1–6 & 19:13–15; *Yeshua is Alive-The Empty Tomb in Jerusalem* based on Matthew 26:17-56, Jn 19:16-20:18, Lk 24:50-53. Ages 3-7, Softcover, 48 pages.

978-1936716685   **LB89** $14.99

To the Ends of the Earth – How the First Jewish Followers of Yeshua Transformed the Ancient World
— Dr. Jeffrey Seif

Everyone knows that the first followers of Yeshua were Jews, and that Christianity was very Jewish for the first 50 to 100 years. It's a known fact that there were many congregations made up mostly of Jews, although the false perception today is, that in the second century they disappeared. Dr. Seif reveals the truth of what happened to them and how these early Messianic Jews influenced and transformed the behavior of the known world at that time.

978-1936716463   **LB83** $17.99

Passion for Israel: *A Short History of the Evangelical Church's Support of Israel and the Jewish People*
—Dan Juster

History reveals a special commitment of Christians to the Jews as God's still elect people, but the terrible atrocities committed against the Jews by so-called Christians have overshadowed the many good deeds that have been performed. This important history needs to be told to help heal the wounds and to inspire more Christians to stand together in support of Israel.

978-1936716401   **LB78** $9.99

Jewish Roots and Foundations of the Scriptures I
—John Fischer, Th.D, Ph.D.

An outstanding evangelical leader once said: "There is something shallow about a Christianity that has lost its Jewish roots." A beautiful painting is a careful interweaving of a number of elements. Among other things, there are the background, the foreground and the subject. Discovering the roots of your faith is a little like appreciating the various parts of a painting. In the background is the panorama of preparation and pictures found in the Old Testament. In the foreground is the landscape and light of the first century Jewish setting. All of this is intricately connected with and highlights the subject—which becomes the flowering of all these aspects—the coming of God to earth and what that means for us. Discovering and appreciating your roots in this way broadens, deepens and enriches your faith and your understanding of Scripture. This audio is 32 hours of live class instruction - audio is clear and easy to understand.

9781936716623　　**LCD03**　$49.99

The Gospels in their Jewish Context
—John Fischer, Th.D, Ph.D.

An examination of the Jewish background and nature of the Gospels in their contemporary political, cultural and historical settings, emphasizing each gospel's special literary presentation of Yeshua, and highlighting the cultural and religious contexts necessary for understanding each of the gospels. 32 hours of audio/video instruction on MP3-DVD and pdf of syllabus.

978-1936716241　　**LCD01**　$49.99

The Epistles from a Jewish Perspective
—John Fischer, Th.D, Ph.D.

An examination of the relationship of Rabbi Shaul (the Apostle Paul) and the Apostles to their Jewish contemporaries and environment; surveys their Jewish practices, teaching, controversy with the religious leaders, and many critical passages, with emphasis on the Jewish nature, content, and background of these letters. 32 hours of audio/video instruction on MP3-DVD and pdf of syllabus.

978-1936716258　　**LCD02**　$49.99

The Red Heifer *A Jewish Cry for Messiah*
—Anthony Cardinale

Award-winning journalist and playwright Anthony Cardinale has traveled extensively in Israel, and recounts here his interviews with Orthodox rabbis, secular Israelis, and Palestinian Arabs about the current search for a red heifer by Jewish radicals wishing to rebuild the Temple and bring the Messiah. These real-life interviews are interwoven within an engaging and dramatic fictional portrayal of the diverse people of Israel and how they would react should that red heifer be found. Readers will find themselves in the Land, where they can hear learned rabbis and ordinary Israelis talking about the red heifer and dealing with all the related issues and the imminent coming and identity of Messiah.

978-1936716470　　LB79　　$19.99

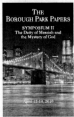

The Borough Park Papers
—Multiple Authors

As you read the New Testament, you "overhear" debates first-century Messianic Jews had about critical issues, e.g. Gentiles being "allowed" into the Messianic kingdom (Acts 15). Similarly, you're now invited to "listen in" as leading twenty-first century Messianic Jewish theologians discuss critical issues facing us today. Some ideas may not fit into your previously held pre-suppositions or pre-conceptions. Indeed, you may find some paradigm shifting in your thinking. We want to share the thoughts of these thinkers with you, our family in the Messiah.

Symposium I:
The Gospel and the Jewish People
248 pages

978-1936716593	LB84	$39.95

Symposium II:
The Deity of Messiah and the Mystery of God
211 pages

978-1936716609	LB85	$39.95

Symposium III:
How Jewish Should the Messianic Community Be?

978-1936716616	LB86	$39.95

On The Way to Emmaus: *Searching the Messianic Prophecies*
—Dr. Jacques Doukhan

An outstanding compilation of the most critical Messianic prophecies by a renowned conservative Christian Scholar, drawing on material from the Bible, Rabbinic sources, Dead Sea Scrolls, and more.

978-1936716432	LB80	$14.99

Yeshua *A Guide to the Real Jesus and the Original Church*
—Dr. Ron Moseley

Opens up the history of the Jewish roots of the Christian faith. Illuminates the Jewish background of Yeshua and the Church and never flinches from showing "Jesus was a Jew, who was born, lived, and died, within first century Judaism." Explains idioms in the New Testament. Endorsed by Dr. Brad Young and Dr. Marvin Wilson. 213 pages.

978-1880226681	**LB29**	$12.99

Gateways to Torah *Joining the Ancient Conversation on the Weekly Portion*
—Rabbi Russell Resnik

From before the days of Messiah until today, Jewish people have read from and discussed a prescribed portion of the Pentateuch each week. Now, a Messianic Jewish Rabbi, Russell Resnik, brings another perspective on the Torah, that of a Messianic Jew. 246 pages.

978-1880226889	**LB42**	$15.99

Creation to Completion *A Guide to Life's Journey from the Five Books of Moses*
—Rabbi Russell Resnik

Endorsed by Coach Bill McCartney, Founder of Promise Keepers & Road to Jerusalem: "Paul urged Timothy to study the Scriptures (2 Tim. 3:16), advising him to apply its teachings to all aspects of his life. Since there was no New Testament then, this rabbi/apostle was convinced that his disciple would profit from studying the Torah, the Five Books of Moses, and the Old Testament. Now, Rabbi Resnik has written a warm devotional commentary that will help you understand and apply the Law of Moses to your life in a practical way." 256 pages

978-1880226322	**LB61**	$14.99

Walk Genesis! Walk Exodus! Walk Leviticus! Walk Numbers! Walk Deuteronomy!
Messianic Jewish Devotional Commentaries
—Jeffrey Enoch Feinberg, Ph.D.

Using the weekly synagogue readings, Dr. Jeffrey Feinberg has put together some very valuable material in his "Walk" series. Each section includes a short Hebrew lesson (for the non-Hebrew speaker), key concepts, an excellent overview of the portion, and some practical applications. Can be used as a daily devotional as well as a Bible study tool.

Walk Genesis!	238 pages	978-1880226759	**LB34**	$12.99
Walk Exodus!	224 pages	978-1880226872	**LB40**	$12.99
Walk Leviticus!	208 pages	978-1880226926	**LB45**	$12.99
Walk Numbers!	211 pages	978-1880226995	**LB48**	$12.99
Walk Deuteronomy!	231 pages	978-1880226186	**LB51**	$12.99
SPECIAL! Five-book Walk!		5 Book Set **Save $10**	**LK28**	$54.99

Good News According To Matthew
—Dr. Henry Einspruch

English translation with quotations from the Tanakh (Old Testament) capitalized and printed in Hebrew. Helpful notations are included. Lovely black and white illustrations throughout the book. 86 pages.

| | 978-1880226025 | **LB03** | $4.99 |
| Also available in Yiddish. | | **LB02** | $4.99 |

They Loved the Torah *What Yeshua's First Followers Really Thought About the Law*
—Dr. David Friedman

Although many Jews believe that Paul taught against the Law, this book disproves that notion. An excellent case for his premise that all the first followers of the Messiah were not only Torah-observant, but also desired to spread their love for God's entire Word to the gentiles to whom they preached. 144 pages. Endorsed by Dr. David Stern, Ariel Berkowitz, Rabbi Dr. Stuart Dauermann & Dr. John Fischer.

| | 978-1880226940 | **LB47** | $9.99 |

The Distortion *2000 Years of Misrepresenting the Relationship Between Jesus the Messiah and the Jewish People*
—Dr. John Fischer & Dr. Patrice Fischer

Did the Jews kill Jesus? Did they really reject him? With the rise of global anti–Semitism, it is important to understand what the Gospels teach about the relationship between Jewish people and their Messiah. 2000 years of distortion have made this difficult. Learn how the distortion began and continues to this day and what you can do to change it. 126 pages. Endorsed by Dr. Ruth Fleischer, Rabbi Russell Resnik, Dr. Daniel C. Juster, Dr. Michael Rydelnik.

| | 978-1880226254 | **LB54** | $11.99 |

---

eBooks Now Available!
All books are available as ebooks for your favorite reader

Visit www.messianicjewish.net for direct links to these readers for each available eBook.

God's Appointed Times *A Practical Guide to Understanding and Celebrating the Biblical Holidays* – **New Edition.**

—Rabbi Barney Kasdan

The Biblical Holy Days teach us about the nature of God and his plan for mankind, and can be a source of God's blessing for all believers–Jews and Gentiles–today. Includes historical background, traditional Jewish observance, New Testament relevance, and prophetic significance, plus music, crafts and holiday recipes. 145 pages.

English	978-1880226353	**LB63**	$12.99
Spanish	978-1880226391	**LB59**	$12.99

God's Appointed Customs *A Messianic Jewish Guide to the Biblical Lifecycle and Lifestyle*

— Rabbi Barney Kasdan

Explains how biblical customs are often the missing key to unlocking the depths of Scripture. Discusses circumcision, the Jewish wedding, and many more customs mentioned in the New Testament. Companion to *God's Appointed Times*. 170 pages.

English	978-1880226636	**LB26**	$12.99
Spanish	978-1880226551	**LB60**	$12.99

Celebrations of the Bible *A Messianic Children's Curriculum*

Did you know that each Old Testament feast or festival finds its fulfillment in the New? They enrich the lives of people who experience and enjoy them. Our popular curriculum for children is in a brand new, user-friendly format. The lay-flat at binding allows you to easily reproduce handouts and worksheets. Celebrations of the Bible has been used by congregations, Sunday schools, ministries, homeschoolers, and individuals to teach children about the biblical festivals. Each of these holidays are presented for Preschool (2-K), Primary (Grades 1-3), Junior (Grades 4-6), and Children's Worship/Special Services. 208 pages.

978-1880226261	**LB55**	$24.99

Passover: *The Key That Unlocks the Book of Revelation*

—Daniel C. Juster, Th.D.

Is there any more enigmatic book of the Bible than Revelation? Controversy concerning its meaning has surrounded it back to the first century. Today, the arguments continue. Yet, Dan Juster has given us the key that unlocks the entire book—the events and circumstances of the Passover/Exodus. By interpreting Revelation through the lens of Exodus, Dan Juster provides a unified overview that helps us read Revelation as it was always meant to be read, as a drama of spiritual conflict, deliverance, and above all, worship. He also shows how this final drama, fulfilled in Messiah, resonates with the Torah and all of God's Word. — Russ Resnik, Executive Director, Union of Messianic Jewish Congregations.

978-1936716210	**LB74**	$10.99

The Messianic Passover Haggadah
Revised and Updated
—Rabbi Barry Rubin and Steffi Rubin.

Guides you through the traditional Passover seder dinner, step-by-step. Not only does this observance remind us of our rescue from Egyptian bondage, but, we remember Messiah's last supper, a Passover seder. The theme of redemption is seen throughout the evening. What's so unique about our Haggadah is the focus on Yeshua (Jesus) the Messiah and his teaching, especially on his last night in the upper room. 36 pages.

English	978-1880226292	**LB57**	$4.99
Spanish	978-1880226599	**LBSP01**	$4.99

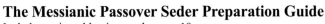

The Messianic Passover Seder Preparation Guide
Includes recipes, blessings and songs. 19 pages.

English	978-1880226247	**LB10**	$2.99
Spanish	978-1880226728	**LBSP02**	$2.99

The Sabbath *Entering God's Rest*
—Barry Rubin & Steffi Rubin

Even if you've never celebrated Shabbat before, this book will guide you into the rest God has for all who would enter in—Jews and non-Jews. Contains prayers, music, recipes; in short, everything you need to enjoy the Sabbath, even how to observe havdalah, the closing ceremony of the Sabbath. Also discusses the Saturday or Sunday controversy. 48 pages.

978-1880226742	**LB32**	$6.99

Havdalah *The Ceremony that Completes the Sabbath*
—Dr. Neal & Jamie Lash

The Sabbath ends with this short, yet equally sweet ceremony called havdalah (separation). This ceremony reminds us to be a light and a sweet fragrance in this world of darkness as we carry the peace, rest, joy and love of the Sabbath into the work week. 28 pages.

978-1880226605	**LB69**	$4.99

Dedicate and Celebrate!
A Messianic Jewish Guide to Hanukkah
—Barry Rubin & Family

Hanukkah means "dedication" — a theme of significance for Jews and Christians. Discussing its historical background, its modern-day customs, deep meaning for all of God's people, this little book covers all the how-tos! Recipes, music, and prayers for lighting the menorah, all included! 32 pages.

978-1880226834	**LB36**	$4.99

The Conversation
An Intimate Journal of the Emmaus Encounter
—Judy Salisbury

"Then beginning with Moses and with all the prophets, He explained to them the things concerning Himself in all the Scriptures." Luke 24:27
If you've ever wondered what that conversation must have been like, this captivating book takes you there.
"The Conversation brings to life that famous encounter between the two disciples and our Lord Jesus on the road to Emmaus. While it is based in part on an imaginative reconstruction, it is filled with the throbbing pulse of the excitement of the sensational impact that our Lord's resurrection should have on all of our lives." ~ Dr. Walter Kaiser President Emeritus Gordon-Conwell Theological Seminary. Hardcover 120 pages.

Hardcover	978-1936716173	**LB73**	$14.99
Paperback	978-1936716364	**LB77**	$9.99

Growing to Maturity
A Messianic Jewish Discipleship Guide
—Daniel C. Juster, Th.D.

This discipleship series presents first steps of understanding and spiritual practice, tailored for the Jewish believer. It's purpose is to aid the believer in living according to Yeshua's will as a disciple, one who has learned the example of his teacher. The course is structured according to recent advances in individualized educational instruction. Discipleship is serious business and the material is geared for serious study and reflection. Each chapter is divided into short sections followed by study questions. 256 pages.

978-1936716227	**LB75**	$19.99

Growing to Maturity Primer: *A Messianic Jewish Discipleship Workbook*
—Daniel C. Juster, Th.D.

A basic book of material in question and answer form. Usable by everyone. 60 pages.

978-0961455507	**TB16**	$7.99

Proverbial Wisdom & Common Sense
—Derek Leman

A Messianic Jewish Approach to Today's Issues from the Proverbs Unique in style and scope, this commentary on the book of Proverbs, written in devotional style, is divided into chapters suitable for daily reading. A virtual encyclopedia of practical advice on family, sex, finances, gossip, honesty, love, humility, and discipline. Endorsed by Dr. John Walton, Dr. Jeffrey Feinberg and Rabbi Barney Kasdan. 248 pages.

978-1880226780	**LB35**	$14.99

That They May Be One *A Brief Review of Church Restoration Movements and Their Connection to the Jewish People*
—Daniel Juster, Th.D

Something prophetic and momentous is happening. The Church is finally fully grasping its relationship to Israel and the Jewish people. Author describes the restoration movements in Church history and how they connected to Israel and the Jewish people. Each one contributed in some way—some more, some less—toward the ultimate unity between Jews and Gentiles. Predicted in the Old Testament and fulfilled in the New, Juster believes this plan of God finds its full expression in Messianic Judaism. He may be right. See what you think as you read *That They May Be One*. 100 pages.

| | 978-1880226711 | **LB71** | $9.99 |

The Greatest Commandment
How the Sh'ma Leads to More Love in Your Life
—Irene Lipson

"What is the greatest commandment?" Yeshua was asked. His reply—"Hear, O Israel, the Lord our God, the Lord is one, and you are to love Adonai your God with all your heart, with all your soul, with all your understanding, and all your strength." A superb book explaining each word so the meaning can be fully grasped and lived. Endorsed by Elliot Klayman, Susan Perlman, & Robert Stearns. 175 pages.

| | 978-1880226360 | **LB65** | $12.99 |

Blessing the King of the Universe
Transforming Your Life Through the Practice of Biblical Praise
—Irene Lipson

Insights into the ancient biblical practice of blessing God are offered clearly and practically. With examples from Scripture and Jewish tradition, this book teaches the biblical formula used by men and women of the Bible, including the Messiah; points to new ways and reasons to praise the Lord; and explains more about the Jewish roots of the faith. Endorsed by Rabbi Barney Kasdan, Dr. Mitch Glaser, & Rabbi Dr. Dan Cohn-Sherbok. 144 pages.

| | 978-1880226797 | **LB53** | $11.99 |

You Bring the Bagels, I'll Bring the Gospel
Sharing the Messiah with Your Jewish Neighbor
Revised Edition—Now with Study Questions
—Rabbi Barry Rubin

This "how-to-witness-to-Jewish-people" book is an orderly presentation of everything you need to share the Messiah with a Jewish friend. Includes Messianic prophecies, Jewish objections to believing, sensitivities in your witness, words to avoid. A "must read" for all who care about the Jewish people. Good for individual or group study. Used in Bible schools. Endorsed by Harold A. Sevener, Dr. Walter C. Kaiser, Dr. Erwin J. Kolb and Dr. Arthur F. Glasser. 253 pages.

| English | 978-1880226650 | **LB13** | $12.99 |
| Te Tengo Buenas Noticias | 978-0829724103 | **OBSP02** | $14.99 |

Making Eye Contact With God
A Weekly Devotional for Women
—Terri Gillespie

What kind of eyes do you have? Are they downcast and sad? Are they full of God's joy and passion? See yourself through the eyes of God. Using real life anecdotes, combined with scripture, the author reveals God's heart for women everywhere, as she softly speaks of the ways in which women see God. Endorsed by prominent authors: Dr. Angela Hunt, Wanda Dyson and Kathryn Mackel. 247 pages, hardcover.

978-1880226513   **LB68** $19.99

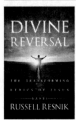

Divine Reversal
The Transforming Ethics of Jesus
—Rabbi Russell Resnik

In the Old Testament, God often reversed the plans of man. Yeshua's ethics continue this theme. Following his path transforms one's life from within, revealing the source of true happiness, forgiveness, reconciliation, fidelity and love. From the introduction, "As a Jewish teacher, Jesus doesn't separate matters of theology from practice. His teaching is consistently practical, ethical, and applicable to real life, even two thousand years after it was originally given." Endorsed by Jonathan Bernis, Dr. Daniel C. Juster, Dr. Jeffrey L. Seif, and Dr Darrell Bock. 206 pages

978-1880226803   **LB72** $12.99

Praying Like the Jew, Jesus
Recovering the Ancient Roots of New Testament Prayer
—Dr. Timothy P. Jones

This eye-opening book reveals the Jewish background of many of Yeshua's prayers. Historical vignettes "transport" you to the times of Yeshua so you can grasp the full meaning of Messiah's prayers. Unique devotional thoughts and meditations, presented in down-to-earth language, provide inspiration for a more meaningful prayer life and help you draw closer to God. Endorsed by Mark Galli, James W. Goll, Rev. Robert Stearns, James F. Strange, and Dr. John Fischer. 144 pages.

978-1880226285   **LB56** $9.99

Growing Your Olive Tree Marriage *A Guide for Couples from Two Traditions*
—David J. Rudolph

One partner is Jewish; the other is Christian. Do they celebrate Hanukkah, Christmas or both? Do they worship in a church or a synagogue? How will the children be raised? This is the first book from a biblical perspective that addresses the concerns of intermarried couples, offering a godly solution. Includes highlights of interviews with intermarried couples. Endorsed by Walter C. Kaiser, Jr., Rabbi Dan Cohn-Sherbok, Jonathan Settel, Dr. Mitchell Glaser & Natalie Sirota. 224 pages.

978-1880226179   **LB50** $12.99

In Search of the Silver Lining *Where is God in the Midst of Life's Storms?*
—Jerry Gramckow

When faced with suffering, what are your choices? Storms have always raged. And people have either perished in their wake or risen above the tempests, shaping history by their responses…new storms are on the horizon. How will we deal with them? How will we shape history or those who follow us? The answer lies in how we view God in the midst of the storms. Endorsed by Joseph C. Aldrich, Ray Beeson, Dr. Daniel Juster. 176 pages.

978-1880226865   **LB39** $10.99

The Voice of the Lord *Messianic Jewish Daily Devotional*
—Edited by David J. Rudolph

Brings insight into the Jewish Scriptures—both Old and New Testaments. Twenty-two prominent Messianic contributors provide practical ways to apply biblical truth. Start your day with this unique resource. Explanatory notes. Perfect companion to the Complete Jewish Bible (see page 2). Endorsed by Edith Schaeffer, Dr. Arthur F. Glaser, Dr. Michael L. Brown, Mitch Glaser and Moishe Rosen. 416 pages.

9781880226704   **LB31** $19.99

Kingdom Relationships *God's Laws for the Community of Faith*
—Dr. Ron Moseley

Dr. Ron Moseley's Yeshua: A Guide to the Real Jesus and the Original Church has taught thousands of people about the Jewishness of not only Yeshua, but of the first followers of the Messiah.

In this work, Moseley focuses on the teaching of Torah -- the Five Books of Moses -- tapping into truths that greatly help modern-day members of the community of faith.

The first section explains the relationship of both the Jewish people and Christians to the Kingdom of God. The second section lists the laws that are applicable to a non-Jew living in the twenty-first century and outside of the land of Israel.

This book is needed because these little known laws of God's Kingdom were, according to Yeshua, the most salient features of the first-century community of believers. Yeshua even warned that anyone breaking these laws would be least in the Kingdom (Matt. 5:19). Additionally, these laws will be the basis for judgment at the end of every believer's life. 64 pages.

978-1880226841   **LB37** $8.99

Train Up A Child *Successful Parenting For The Next Generation*
—Dr. Daniel L. Switzer

The author, former principal of Ets Chaiyim Messianic Jewish Day School, and father of four, combines solid biblical teaching with Jewish sources on child raising, focusing on the biblical holy days, giving fresh insight into fulfilling the role of parent. 188 pages. Endorsed by Dr. David J. Rudolph, Paul Lieberman, and Dr. David H. Stern.

978-1880226377   **LB64** $12.99

Fire on the Mountain - *Past Renewals, Present Revivals and the Coming Return of Israel*
—Dr. Louis Goldberg

The term "revival" is often used to describe a person or congregation turning to God. Is this something that "just happens," or can it be brought about? Dr. Louis Goldberg, author and former professor of Hebrew and Jewish Studies at Moody Bible Institute, examines real revivals that took place in Bible times and applies them to today. 268 pages.

978-1880226858   **LB38** $15.99

Voices of Messianic Judaism *Confronting Critical Issues Facing a Maturing Movement*
—General Editor Rabbi Dan Cohn-Sherbok

Many of the best minds of the Messianic Jewish movement contributed their thoughts to this collection of 29 substantive articles. Challenging questions are debated: The involvement of Gentiles in Messianic Judaism? How should outreach be accomplished? Liturgy or not? Intermarriage? 256 pages.

978-1880226933   **LB46** $15.99

The Enduring Paradox *Exploratory Essays in Messianic Judaism*
—General Editor Dr. John Fischer

Yeshua and his Jewish followers began a new movement—Messianic Judaism—2,000 years ago. In the 20th century, it was reborn. Now, at the beginning of the 21st century, it is maturing. Twelve essays from top contributors to the theology of this vital movement of God, including: Dr. Walter C. Kaiser, Dr. David H. Stern, and Dr. John Fischer. 196 pages.

978-1880226902   **LB43** $13.99

The World To Come *A Portal to Heaven on Earth*
—Derek Leman

An insightful book, exposing fallacies and false teachings surrounding this extremely important subject... paints a hopeful picture of the future and dispels many non-biblical notions. Intriguing chapters: Magic and Desire, The Vision of the Prophets, Hints of Heaven, Horrors of Hell, The Drama of the Coming Ages. Offers a fresh, but old, perspective on the world to come, as it interacts with the prophets of Israel and the Bible. 110 pages.

978-1880226049   **LB67**   .$9.99

Hebrews Through a Hebrew's Eyes
—Dr. Stuart Sacks

Written to first-century Messianic Jews, this epistle, understood through Jewish eyes, edifies and encourages all. 119 pages. Endorsed by Dr. R.C. Sproul and James M. Boice.

978-1880226612   **LB23** $10.99

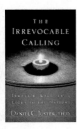

The Irrevocable Calling *Israel's Role As A Light To The Nations*
—Daniel C. Juster, Th.D.

Referring to the chosen-ness of the Jewish people, Paul, the Apostle, wrote "For God's free gifts and his calling are irrevocable" (Rom. 11:29). This messenger to the Gentiles understood the unique calling of his people, Israel. So does Dr. Daniel Juster, President of Tikkun Ministries Int'l. In *The Irrevocable Calling*, he expands Paul's words, showing how Israel was uniquely chosen to bless the world and how these blessings can be enjoyed today. Endorsed by Dr. Jack Hayford, Mike Bickle and Don Finto. 64 pages.

	978-1880226346	**LB66**	$8.99

Are There Two Ways of Atonement?
—Dr. Louis Goldberg

Here Dr. Louis Goldberg, long-time professor of Jewish Studies at Moody Bible Institute, exposes the dangerous doctrine of Two-Covenant Theology. 32 pages.

	978-1880226056	**LB12**	$ 4.99

Awakening *Articles and Stories About Jews and Yeshua*
—Arranged by Anna Portnov

Articles, testimonies, and stories about Jewish people and their relationship with God, Israel, and the Messiah. Includes the effective tract, "The Most Famous Jew of All." One of our best anthologies for witnessing to Jewish people. Let this book witness for you! Russian version also available. 110 pages.

English	978-1880226094	**LB15**	$ 6.99
Russian	978-1880226018	**LB14**	$ 6.99

The Unpromised Land *The Struggle of Messianic Jews Gary and Shirley Beresford*
—Linda Alexander

They felt God calling them to live in Israel, the Promised Land. Wanting nothing more than to live quietly and grow old together in the country of refuge for all Jewish people, little did they suspect what events would follow to try their faith. The fight to make *aliyah*, to claim their rightful inheritance in the Promised Land, became a battle waged not only for themselves, but also for Messianic Jews all over the world that wish to return to the Jewish homeland. Here is the true saga of the Beresford's journey to the land of their forefathers. 216 pages.

	978-1880226568	**LB19**	$ 9.99

Death of Messiah *Twenty fascinating articles that address a subject of grief, hope, and ultimate triumph.*
—Edited by Kai Kjaer-Hansen

This compilation, written by well-known Jewish believers, addresses the issue of Messiah and offers proof that Yeshua—the true Messiah—not only died, but also was resurrected! 160 pages.

978-1880226582   **LB20** $ 8.99

Beloved Dissident *(A Novel)*
—Laurel West

A gripping story of human relationships, passionate love, faith, and spiritual testing. Set in the world of high finance, intrigue, and international terrorism, the lives of David, Jonathan, and Leah intermingle on many levels--especially their relationships with one another and with God. As the two men tangle with each other in a rising whirlwind of excitement and danger, each hopes to win the fight for Leah's love. One of these rivals will move Leah to a level of commitment and love she has never imagined--or dared to dream. Whom will she choose? 256 pages.

978-1880226766   **LB33** $ 9.99

Sudden Terror
—Dr. David Friedman

Exposes the hidden agenda of militant Islam. The author, a former member of the Israel Defense Forces, provides eye-opening information needed in today's dangerous world.
Dr. David Friedman recounts his experiences confronting terrorism; analyzes the biblical roots of the conflict between Israel and Islam; provides an overview of early Islam; demonstrates how the United States and Israel are bound together by a common enemy; and shows how to cope with terrorism and conquer fear. The culmination of many years of research and personal experiences. This expose will prepare you for what's to come! 160 pages.

978-1880226155   **LB49** $ 9.99

It is Good! *Growing Up in a Messianic Family*
—Steffi Rubin

Growing up in a Messianic Jewish family. Meet Tovah! Tovah (Hebrew for "Good") is growing up in a Messianic Jewish home, learning the meaning of God`s special days. Ideal for young children, it teaches the biblical holidays and celebrates faith in Yeshua. 32 pages to read & color.

978-1880226063   **LB11** $ 4.99